#IMOMSOHARD

KRISTIN HENSLEY
AND JEN SMEDLEY

HarperOne
An Imprint of HarperCollinsPublishers

HarperOne

This is a work of nonfiction. The words, experiences, and memories are the authors' alone. Some names in this book have been changed to protect people's privacy.

HarperCollins books may be purchased for educational, business, or sales promotional use. For information, please email the Special Markets Department at SPsales@harpercollins.com.

FIRST EDITION

Designed by Janet Evans-Scanlon

Illustrations by Yvonne Chan

Library of Congress Cataloging-in-Publication Data has been applied for.

ISBN 978-0-06-285769-9
ISBN 978-0-06-295335-3 (Int'l)
ISBN 978-0-06-293752-0 (Target)
ISBN 978-0-06-295329-2 (Walmart and BAM)

19 20 21 22 23 LSC 10 9 8 7 6 5 4 3 2 1

(Raising a glass)

This book is dedicated to:

Finn and Dashiel, the boys who made us moms

*Delilah and Eleanor, our girls,
who may one day be moms*

Our own moms, Terri and Barbara

Our dads, Dewey and Jerry

*And our loving husbands, Brit and Colin,
the official Mom Makers in our lives.*

Most of all, this book is dedicated to all the moms!

*We see you.
We get you.
We love you.*

CONTENTS

CONTENTS

HEY, FRIEND!

We're Kristin and Jen. We are currently typing this on a laptop in a car in a parking garage. There is a bag of ravaged Chipotle next to us. We are text fighting with our husbands. We will be late to pick up the kids. To make matters worse, this laptop was dropped on the way to get the kids in the car this morning, so the space bar is hanging on by a thread. Like us.

Tonight, we will do our best to feed the kids, get them ready for tomorrow, give them love, praise, and encouragement, and wrestle them to bed. We will then put on our comfy pants, which are only getting tighter, clean up the house, and spend five to ten minutes prepping for tomorrow. We will pour a glass of wine, the signal that we are "off duty." Only we are not, of course—a mom is never off the clock. She's simply on call, as at any moment someone could barf, have a nightmare, want to know why people die, or simply think their pajamas feel too "bally" all of a sudden.

Why are we saying "we"? Don't we have our own brain? Sometimes we do. And sometimes we don't feel like we have

one at all. But we're best friends, so we share a brain, or at least similar thoughts, all the time. Since becoming mothers, the thought we share all the time is *Boy, I really suck at this.*

We know we're lucky. For so many reasons. The number one reason is that we have wonderful children, husbands, and families, and we're all okay. But we're also lucky because we have each other to lean on when our children, husbands, and families drive us absolutely bonkers.

We started the web series #IMOMSOHARD because we made each other laugh, and we made each other feel better when we felt like we were really failing at motherhood. We figured that if another mom saw the terrible job that we were doing, she might feel better about the job that she's doing. When you're up all night breastfeeding or taking care of a sick kid, you can find a lot of stuff online that tells you how to improve upon the job you're doing, or how tragedy can strike you or your innocent child at any moment. Real depressing stuff. No thanks.

The truth is, you don't need advice; you need understanding. Because there's nothing like feeling alone and then hearing that someone else is going through the same mess you are. We've done it for each other, and we want to do the same for you. So here's the stuff we like to talk about when we get together. It makes us laugh. It makes us feel better. Hopefully it will do the same for you. Because you're not alone. While you read, you're off duty for a few minutes. Pour yourself a glass of wine and have a little "me" time with we. (Unless you're reading this in the bathroom, as moms often must. Then have a little wee-wee time with us.)

LOVE, KRISTIN & JEN

WE INTRODUCE OURSELVES SO HARD

Before we get started, let us tell you how we got the idea to #I MOM SO HARD.

We both lived in Nebraska through college, but we never found each other even though it's not heavily populated and you can see for a hundred miles in every direction. We had all the same friends. We were studying the same subjects, and we went to all the same bars. Kristin's roommate was even in an improv group with Jen, and yet we never met. It was like *Sliding Doors*, but with more Cornhuskers gear. A bunch of near misses.

After college, we both moved hundreds of miles away from Nebraska and somehow ended up only a block apart from each other in California. Not that we knew it, though. We were doing all the same things, had all the same friends, and we *still* never met. We weren't total twinsies—Jen was into weird witchy shit (she's not a Wiccan or anything, but she believes in crystals and stuff) and felt naked without jewelry, and Kristin was more of a tomboy—but it is insane that the stars didn't align and arrange a meet-cute for us.

And then one day, the universe caught us. We found ourselves outside a small, weird theater that used to be a hair salon, drinking brews in the parking lot, which was a welcome throwback to our Nebraska days, minus the banging sounds of Warrant. Even that night, it took us a while to meet. We kept circling and narrowly missing each other, until, finally, we were back-to-back loud-talking to different people about Nebraska. We both turned to each other in unison and said, "Wait. You're from Nebraska?"

Now imagine a Rolodex flipping really, really fast as we shouted out the names of every single person that we knew in common. It was like we were mad at each other:

Jen: **KRISTY SCHWEDE?!**

Kristin: **I WENT TO SCHOOL WITH HER!
HOW DO YOU KNOW HER?!**

Jen: **WE BOTH WORKED AT TGI FRIDAYS!**

Kristin: **CARRIE SMILEWOOD?**

Jen: **YES!**

Kristin: **NO!**

Jen: **SHE'S BEEN MY BEST FRIEND SINCE
WE WERE LIKE 15!**

Kristin: **MICHELLE ASHLEY?**

Jen: **I DID IMPROV WITH HER!**

Kristin: **SHE'S MY ROOMMATE!**

Jen: **NUH-UH!**

Kristin: **YES-HUH!**

Jen: **I WAS AT HER GRADUATION PARTY!**

Kristin: **I *THREW* THAT PARTY!**

We exchanged phone numbers and started hanging out a day or two later. We just began in the middle. It was like we didn't have time to pussyfoot around, so we acted like we'd known each other all along. We got each other right from the beginning. You know when you're a little kid and you would stare awkwardly at the kid in front of you and ask, "Do you want to be my friend?" And that kid would say, "Yes," and then you were bound for life? That was us. One of us would call the other and be like, "Hey, I've got Ritz and spray cheese and half a bottle of wine left. You want to come over?" And the other one would say, "Give me five minutes." It felt like being home.

We hung out constantly. We flipped each other's shit, and we laughed. A lot. When you have a friend who can make fun of you for your excessive gray hair—or your lip hair—it's the most wonderful medicine. It takes all the air out of how serious any situation is, and that's what we try to do for each other. We also respected each other, and we celebrated each other's wins. Not everything was a friggin' Hallmark movie or one big Sarah McLachlan song, but for the most part, we had a sense of humor, and we were tougher together.

We met during that "I'm not sure what I'm doing with my life, but I know that I'm doing it wrong" phase of adulthood. If you're single, you start to feel like you should be married. And if you're married, you ask yourself, *Why did I do this to myself?* Because we were both single, we spent most of our time on our careers: Kristin as a teacher and a commercial actor (when the work came), and Jen as a salesperson for skincare products and a writer (when the work came).

We were able to be very patient and understanding with one another because we were both fighting the same good fight: survival. Keeping your car running. Paying your bills. Going to the dentist. Looking happy. You know, the same stuff you try to do now, only while you're also keeping unappreciative children alive.

When we didn't talk for a few weeks, we still picked up from where we had left off. You know those kinds of friends? The ones where you don't have to say, "I've been busy," "I've been sad," "I've been lazy," etc.? You can just say "cheers" and open the floodgates? Everyone needs one of those, and that's who we've been for each other.

Eventually, we both got married. Then we went through pregnancy together, and that sealed the Friends-for-Life deal for us. It's amazing that a friendship can get even deeper after you have kids, but the right mom friend is a lifesaver. Because, let's face it, when you're a new mom, you feel incredibly isolated. You feel so far away from family, from work, from friends. But one of us would call, and before the phone was even hung up, there'd be a knock at the door, and someone who got it would be on the other side. Within minutes, we'd both be crying, both feeling like utter failures, wondering, *Why doesn't anybody tell you it's like this?*

One day, after Jen wiped snot from her chin with the back of her hand, she said, "You know what? We crack each other up. I bet other moms could use a laugh, too."

Between us, we had four small children, zero time and even less energy, and no real plan, so we thought, *Yes*. We wanted to make something for you to watch when you're up in the middle of the night worrying about SIDS or whether you'd seen the *To Catch a Predator* van on your street—something that would cheer you up instead of making you think about how everyone you love will eventually die.

And of course, we did it wrong. We decided we were going to be like talk-show hosts, thinking that if we were super happy and peppy, we'd make other moms happy and peppy. People love Rachael Ray, right? The problem was, peppy was the furthest thing from how we felt.

When we were ready for our first shoot, Kristin had a raging period and cystic acne so big and so covered in blush that it looked like she'd put a clown nose on the wrong part of her face. Jen was sweaty and had on a cardigan that was too tight and too hot. She'd been breastfeeding and was so engorged that her sweater was coming apart—and not in a good way. Her eyes were little slits. You could barely even see them. It was like she'd just lost a fight.

We started filming, and Kristin chirped in her best Kelly Ripa, "Hello!" and introduced herself and her kids. When it was Jen's turn, she introduced herself and said her son's name, and then she froze.

"My daughter's name is . . . [*crickets*]."

SHE HAD FORGOTTEN HER DAUGHTER'S NAME.

It's Delilah. Her daughter's name is Delilah.

In all fairness, Delilah was still attached to Jen all the time, so it wasn't like Jen had started using her name regularly. Delilah wasn't bringing anyone the remote or anything. And, like a really good friend, instead of helping Jen out, Kristin snort-laughed. "You just forgot your kid's name!" She would not let it go.

We didn't even have a full video. But we knew there was something really awesome in Jen forgetting Delilah's name, so we said, "Why the hell not?" and posted it. We got five thousand views in two days, and we said, "Holy moly, there are women commenting on here who we don't even know!" And then we agreed, "That's the sign."

So we did a Mother's Day video. We did one on hemorrhoids, one on the joy of Spanx, one on sex after kids. And no matter what, no matter how peculiar or sad or weird we got, women said, "OMG, me too! I thought I was the only one."

We did a postpartum episode, and we talked about some pretty dark stuff, mostly about anxiety and how Kristin was afraid every time she walked through a doorway that she would hit her son's head on the door and his head would explode, which we're pretty sure would defy the laws of physics or at least carpentry. Doorways terrified her—and do you know how many doorways there are in the world? Every room has at least one! After we posted that video, so many moms were like, "I have that fear too!" Other moms chimed in to say that they were afraid that they were going to fall off a cliff while holding their baby. Or dangle him over a balcony, MJ-style.

We realized that no one was showing the kinds of conversations moms have together in an open, honest way. That's what we do. It's just real real. Real relationships, real women, real love. We make fun of ourselves, not other people. We're not judging anyone. It's not about our kids. We don't want to talk about must-have products or a funny way to put on a Baby-Björn. When we get comments, 90 percent of the time it's "What lipstick are you wearing?" and then it's women tagging a friend because it's the same conversation they'd just been having. No matter how out-there or specific your particular screwup or neurosis is, you're not the only one. It's like porn. There is always someone out there who has the same quirk you do.

The truth is, being a mom is f*cking tough, but it is so much easier when there's someone who understands and has your back. We've got to be there for one another. We've got to love one another, support one another. Because—let's be honest—no matter what we do, the kids are going to blame us for all the stuff that goes wrong in their lives anyway. Nobody's ever in therapy in thirty years going, "Hey, by the way, my mother has nothing to do with why I'm here. She's blameless. Nothing but inspirational."

There's simply no such thing as a perfect mom. You know that mom who seems to have it all together all the time? Who's real happy, who doesn't have someone else's boogers on her face, and who likes to bake things to bring to school when it's not even her day? Let us tell you something: she's bawling in her shower just like the rest of us.

Nobody's got it figured out. You're not the only mom whose kid ate detergent for breakfast. We all just want to do the best job we can do. And if it's not the best job, we're going to be fine with that. We all need to be okay with being just okay some days. You're not alone in this, you guys. You're doing great. Or you're doing good enough—and *that's* great!

Welcome to the party.

I GET KNOCKED UP SO HARD

Let's start at the beginning. Pregnancy feels like you're a victim of a zombie attack. They ate your brains first, and you're the only one afflicted. You're not in control of your body, you lose your ability to think and remember things, and, oh yeah, you're blissfully unaware of what's about to happen to you. You're not fully gone yet—you still remember stuff, you still love your spouse—but all kinds of shocking and gross things start happening. The moment the pregnancy test screams *Pregnant!* a micro-size brass band starts marching in your uterus. Cue excitement, cue barfing, cue fatigue, and cue terror.

The most bizarre part of pregnancy is the first trimester when you don't look any different, and, if you're one of the lucky ones, you don't feel any different. You have to remind yourself that you can't eat sushi or join in at happy hour. It's like a fun little secret that nobody gets to know unless you want them to. You just get to field all the "Are you gaining weight due to gluttony or sloth?" questions.

Pretty soon, the second trimester rolls in, and the fun part starts: sharing the news, showing off a tiny bump, picking out cute stuff for the nursery. You are mobile, you are happy, you are glowing—and then slowly, steadily, the snow globe–size being in your gut grows to the size of an *actual* globe.

Finally, you hit the third trimester, and the magic starts to feel less like magic and more like pain. You can see the baby's foot kicking through your stomach and feel a jab to your rib. *The call is coming from inside the house.* (And the house is your uterus.) Balance is an issue, you haven't seen your labia in weeks (which is shocking because they have enlarged to cocktail wienies), your feet are fat, your thighs hurt, you can't poop, you can't stop peeing, and your boobs are veiny and leaking. It's so uncomfortable that by the time you do deliver it feels like a gift that someone is asking you to shove that globe through your tiny vagina hole. Ah, birth. What a miracle. You are now a *mom-bie*. Welcome! You are now one of the walking dead.

KRISTIN

I was a ginormous giant during my first pregnancy. Fee-fi-fo-fum, I smelled the smell of a Cinnabon. And I ate many. Jen threw a baby shower for me, and we played this game where you run a ribbon around your midsection to see how big your circumference is, and everyone guesses the number. You guys, every single person guessed about ten inches less than my actual number. It was quite a confidence booster. (Years earlier, my husband had made the same mistake when guessing my sexual history, and I'm actually fine with him being that far off the mark.)

My belly was so doughy. Finn had a real luxury condo thing going on in there. When I went in for measurement, my doctors kept using the term "macro-birth." When the doctor first said it, I looked at her like she was asking me to solve a long division problem in my head. I knew that "macro" and "birth" together did not sound awesome. "Macro" means big, and "birth" means something tearing through my vagina, so something big tearing through my vagina sounded, um, carry the one, TERRIFYING.

The docs had a hard time estimating just how big Finn was going to be when he came out, but my husband weighed eleven pounds, and his brothers each weighed twelve at birth. Their mom is six feet tall, so when they asked me at my OB if I wanted to try vaginal birth, I said, "I'm five feet eight. I'll try real hard, but that's going to be a big baby." I should've done that research before choosing a spouse.

I just kept getting bigger, so at forty weeks, my doctors decided we should probably go ahead and induce. I was like, "Great. That's not gonna hurt, is it?" Are you all laughing now?

A few days before the induction was scheduled, we had another appointment. On the way there, I told Colin, "Gosh, this baby's really kicking my chest." It was like a tiny Jackie Chan was having at it right under my chin.

Colin looked at me and said, "The baby is not at your chest, dummy. That's labor."

How did he know? Fair question. Colin might not have had a uterus (still doesn't), but he had read all the books about having one and what happens when you fill one of those babies up with a mini-me. I had read exactly nothing about the miracle that is giving birth. Unless you count fifty "Body after Baby" articles in *Us Weekly*. I was that way my whole pregnancy, but Jen had read all the books, so whenever I had a question and Colin wasn't around, I just asked her for the CliffsNotes version of what was happening to my body. I'd call her, and she'd say, "How are you feeling?"

"Well, I throw up a little bit every time I bend over."

"Totally normal at this gestational age."

And then I'd return to wondering just how big a person could get before you'd end up in a *What's Eating Gilbert Grape* situation. Then I'd go back to eating bagel bites. They were actually just normal bagels that I could eat in one bite. My seventy-pound weight gain is still a mystery.

I took a real "I'll figure it out when I get there" approach to giving birth. I know there are hundreds of books and listicles that can prepare you for what to expect, but that kind of prep is just not my style. Plus, why research when people *love* to give free birthing advice? Everyone had helpful tips, even dudes. One guy told me to rub olive oil "on my holes." He said it would soften the skin. No, I don't know his name, but he does work at Trader Joe's.

I don't read any sort of manuals for the use or maintenance of motor vehicles or small appliances either. I feel like if you can't figure it out by intuition and animal instinct, you just don't need anything that is that complex. Some assembly required? No, thank you. I do not need to be mad all the time, so, Ikea, you can assemble that bookshelf your own self. I am not a carpenter. I paid for it. "Some assembly required" is why

I got married. If it were up to me, my whole house would be decorated with cube furniture and beanbag chairs.

But my husband is a reader and he's Irish, which is a perfect "some assembly required" combo. He loves to put things together, and he loves to know how things work. He likes to come at me with stuff he has read, and a battle of ignorance and education ensues. He'll tell me something like "Did you know that there are more bacteria cells in your body than human cells?"

Me: "That seems made up."

Him: "Nope, that's science."

He'd obviously done his reading about the contractions. When I got to the doctor for the checkup before my induction, they took one look at the monitor and said, "Ma'am, you're already in labor."

My doctor, who is so, so tiny—just super skinny and on a big day is at best five feet tall; I called her a "pocket doctor"—has been delivering babies forever. She came in and did a cervical check, which felt like she was tugging at my esophagus. Her arm was so far up there, I could taste her wedding ring. It felt like she was doing one of those veterinary maneuvers to birth a cow.

"Your tonsils are fine," she joked, and then they told me they were going to break my water.

When they did it, I was sitting on these pads, and fluid just kept coming out. I was looking at everybody saying, "I'm sorry. I'm so sorry," as if I thought someone was going to hand me a mop when it was all over and ask me to please clean up this disgusting mess. Looking back, I wish I hadn't apologized. I wish I would have been amazed at my body's awesomeness. "Look at all of that fluid dumping out of me. I am a pregnancy goddess!"

Anyway, then I labored *forever*. They put me on Pitocin, and it was the worst. I was having contractions every sixteen seconds with no epidural. My saving grace was my labor and delivery coach. I loved her so much. She was so calm, like a beautiful angel sent to remind me that I was not going to be the first woman in the world to have someone watch poop come out of my butthole while I pushed. She mattered more to me than anyone in that room—and my husband was there.

I tried to stay calm, but I knew that even though I was trying to keep it together, I actually looked like a sweaty landlord. I was very conscious that I was not my best self. There were so damn many people in that room. It was like a boy band rehearsal in there. Believe it or not, I am a little shy. I also don't like going to the doctor where the phrase "warts and all" can be applied literally. Usually, before I go to the OB, there's a lot of prep work. It's like going to an auto show. I clean it, polish it, and get out the lint roller. But because I had been counting on a few more days until I was induced, let's just say I was a little unkempt, and the whole team had full access to my problem area hairs. Finally, the pain got to me and I broke. My apologies for sullying the labor and delivery room floor gave way to an angry growl, "You get that f*cking anesthesiologist in here now."

The doctor and the nurses were super calm as they told me, "Kristin, the anesthesiologist is helping another woman." At this point I couldn't stop barfing.

I yelled, *"WHY DOES SHE GET TO GO FIRST?"* Let's be truthful here. I believe my actual words were, "Why does that bitch get to go first?" which I regret. She was in pain too. But I'm positive mine was worse.

14

They slowly backed away like you do when you encounter a crazy person outside the bank as I demanded through a very tight jaw, "Listen, you get him in here. You get him in here *noooowwwwww*!" This, by the way, was good practice for the way I would speak to my son for the first five years of his life.

Then the anesthesiologist came in. I'm not very good with needles and I'm not very good with pain. But my husband is *really* not good with needles and *really* not very good with pain. Colin was so freaked out. When they gave me that pillow to hold so that I could stay still while they jammed a Capri Sun straw into my spinal column, my husband, God love him, was very controlled. I just looked at Colin, as his face went from white to gray. I told him, "Get your head in the game, Sweeney. You don't get to pass out. You stay in this. Don't you go anywhere."

He started looking at me really hard. I could see a little pink come back into his face. But I could also see him sweeping the room for an escape. I told him, "I will get out of this, and I will murder you if you leave me right now." He stayed in there like a champ.

Suddenly, it felt like my back was burning. The epidural didn't work. They had missed. Bro, you had *one job*. How do you screw that up?

My doctor came in and said, "There's a problem," which I don't like hearing when I'm in line at Chipotle, so hearing it while I was on the verge of bringing life into this world did not sit well with me. But I didn't even have a second to spiral out because they hit the go button for a C-section. Instantly, I was wheeled into another room and shrouded in a pop-up tent, separating the upper half of my body from the lower half. I felt like a magician's assistant, and I hate magicians. I have no idea if

15

Colin stayed upright during the surgery, those doctors wouldn't tell me, but a few minutes later, I had my perfect little baby boy. When I saw Finn for the first time, he had so much hair he looked like *ER*-era George Clooney—and he was so pink. And big. And perfect. But most of all when I looked at him he made perfect sense: *There you are, Finn.*

Afterward, there was a big part of me that was disappointed that I didn't have a vaginal birth. If I had just tried a little longer than *twenty-eight hours.* I wanted that experience so badly. I wanted to know what it felt like to push him out the way I was wired to do. It was terribly disappointing. But then I realized how silly I was being. I had a perfect baby, and I didn't blow out my vagina. (But I did blow out my cervix, so there's a little foreshadowing of my birth story about Eleanor.)

FYI, I still haven't read the manual. I just call Jen.

JEN

I've also been seated in section C. Twice.

You hear about celebrities scheduling Cs like they're no big whoop—sort of like you schedule a Brazilian blowout. But if you haven't had one, ladies, let me tell you, they are *brutal.*

The closest thing I can compare my son's birth experience to is an alien abduction. I boarded a sterile ship and was too scared to sleep for forty hours. These crabby green aliens kept coming in and shoving their gloved claws into my hoo-ha every half hour, while they had me hooked to all these machines and video games. They denied me food or drink, tied me to a table, sawed me in half, and ripped a parasite out of me. When it was over, they put this little miniature succubus on me that I'd have to take care of for the next eighteen years. And David Duchovny wasn't even there.

I tried to make a plan for my delivery persona. I didn't want to be one of those stereotypical women in labor. You know, like in the movies, like *Look Who's Talking Too,* where the couple is panicking in the back of the cab, and the mom is yelling things at her poor, beleaguered husband: "I'm gonna kill you! You did this to me!"

You know what? I didn't need to worry. It is not *at all* like the movies, because the movies last two hours and labor lasts two days.

Before we got to the hospital, I had been doing fine. As I was in triage, I could hear another woman screaming down the hall, and I thought, *Yikes, I do not feel like* that.

And then I went from zero to ten on the pain scale in less than a minute. I was just swallowed by pain. When things got real, I went silent.

I just stopped talking. My husband, Brit, was like, "Um, does it hurt?" He was trying to remind me to breathe, and I said, "It hurts between my neck and my feet, but I don't know where." I just blew all my fuses.

This came as a surprise. I've got a high pain threshold because I have an older brother. You'll only understand that if you have an older brother. You need to be able to take a punch without flinching. So I was shocked to find out that, twenty-four hours into labor, simply making eye contact with someone was enough to make me scream.

17

When at last it came time to push, my doctor was very old-school. He told me, "You can't have your epidural while you're pushing, because you can't control your body."

He had that right. If I could control my body, contractions would have felt like hugs from a baby panda, but instead they felt like someone was punching me in the face and the vagina at the same time.

I pushed for two hours, and it didn't do anything. Now, I enjoy many things, you guys—a glass of merlot, a Stevie Nicks acoustic version, books about serial killers—but physical exertion is not among them. For me, pushing for two hours was the equivalent of doing one of those ultramarathons where they run barefoot for days, only everyone was staring at my vagina as I did it. I had no idea what they were seeing down there. I mean, I know from looking in the mirror that my nose can look kind of funny from the right side, but down there? No clue.

The doctors were using all kinds of tools: the speculum, the gloves, the occasional face guard, which, okay, fellas, was a little much, don't you think?

They thought the baby might be sunny-side up. This awful woman, literally the worst nurse on the planet—I was fully prepared to write a strongly worded letter, but I was on too many meds—said, "I'm going to put your leg up on this thing, 'cause it'll turn the baby." She started to manipulate my legs like a physical trainer (note: all of my knowledge of what physical trainers do comes from the *Real Housewives* franchise, not from any real-life experience). Now, I've never heard another woman say, "My labor was pretty rough, but then I just threw my leg in the air and out popped the baby!" so as soon as she lifted my thigh, I said, "This is not a thing that works. Because if this was a thing that worked, they would put legs up all the time, but in real life people end up having to do C-sections."

Suddenly, my midwestern roots took hold, and I was like, "Oh no, I'm being rude." I'm absolutely one of those women who would have died in labor in pioneer days because I would have been scrubbing down the larder with lye while I was laboring because I didn't want to trouble anyone, and then next thing you'd know, I'd be dead, with a baby half out of me.

But before I could say I was sorry for being rude, I let out a string of what people used to call cuss words in the '80s. It seemed that all polite bets were off. I went from "Sorry for my rudeness" to "Back it up. If I want ice chips, I better get some shit-damn-mothafuckin' ice chips. Please." (Of course I still said "please." I was in pain, but I wasn't an animal.)

I made that nurse go get my doctor, who, by the way, was passing kidney stones as I was laboring. If there's such a thing as method acting for doctors, this was it. He wouldn't take any pain meds, because he still wanted to be able to be on call. He came in, took a look, and then went, "The baby's fine. Keep pushing." I kept pushing, nothing worked. An hour later, he goes, "You're gonna have a lot more pushing to do."

Brit turned to him and asked, "When you say 'a lot more,' Doc, what does that mean exactly?"

The doctor said, "Well, it's like we've asked her to do a hundred of her best push-ups, and we're gonna ask her to do a hundred more."

Brit had known me for five years at that time, and as a keen observer of human behavior, knew I had worked out precisely zero times in those years, so without even checking in with me, he goes, "Can she have the C-section?" That was the closest I'd come to wanting to have sex with him in months.

They sped me down to surgery while Brit scrubbed up. They started my anesthesia, and I was already so tired I could barely stay awake. I was so excited but every part of me was exhausted. It felt like the prep and surgery took forever. The surgery team chatted casually, listened to a playlist on someone's iPod and debated over who the musician was that was currently playing, and nearly ripped me off the table removing my new baby boy. *It's Eric Clapton, you idiots*, I thought, too drugged up to speak.

And then I heard crying. A perfect, healthy baby. A tiny living creature who I could not believe they handed to me, trusted me with, and then let me take home. How reckless is that? I still can't believe it sometimes.

I didn't just survive an alien abduction. I freaking brought a new *human being* into this world. *I made a life*. A new little person who will have thoughts and feelings and heartbreak and will experience joy and wonder, and, it's a blasted miracle. How do you like that, entire universe?

They wheeled his plastic, hospital baby holder next to me in recovery, and my arms ached to hold him. After that much work, I could only cry (and shake violently, evidently). I used all my energy to flop my hand onto the side of his crib. Believe it or not, and I will die remembering this moment, Dash reached up and set his tiny baby hand on top of mine.

He was a wish, and then there he was. I had no idea how much happiness that little bald ET of a person would bring me in the coming years, how many times my mind would be blown by his smile, or how watching him hold his sister's hand would make me feel better than any drug I'd ever taken. All I knew was that I had done it. I might have expelled enough liquids onto the hospital floor to require a hazmat team, but I made a baby. And I'm not apologizing to anyone.

I HOMETOWN SO HARD

When you grow up in the Midwest, you are taught (1) that you are only as good as your word, (2) to approach everything with a little common sense, and (3) to trust your gut. Oh, and never show up to a party without a Crock-Pot, a coozie, and a case of beer.

Maybe it's because we farm the land that we are more "grounded" as people. Maybe it's because the seasons are rough, so we appreciate when the weather changes because it's a constant reminder that time passes, so get busy living. Or maybe it's because the Midwest prides itself on the importance of community, faith, and optimism in a way that feels like a warm, heavy quilt.

Who's homesick? You're homesick.

The Midwest takes heat for being frumpy or uneducated or for being made up of flyover states or whatever, but we call BS on all that. The Midwest is like the mom of the US: hardworking, warm, underappreciated, and strong as hell.

KRISTIN

I grew up in a small farming town called Central City. I always thought "Central City" sounded fancy, like a place where a superhero would live when she's not out saving the world, but it's actually just a quiet hamlet with beautiful farmland and easygoing people. It boasts a population of about 2,500, give or take a cousin. It's a town full of the finest people you will ever meet. Good people. Solid people. The kind of people who don't care how much you have or don't have. They will always ask you the same two questions: "How are your folks?" and "Can I buy you a beer?"

Nebraskans are so, so warm. My husband found himself in central Nebraska at the Husker Harvest Days a while back, and when he told me about it he said, "Of all the places I've traveled in the country, Nebraskans are the nicest." (I appreciated the compliment so much that I put out that night just to drive the point home.)

When I lived there, Central City had a Dairy Queen, a Subway, and sometimes a Pizza Hut. There was one small grocery store, which we referred to as "the mall." We had three stoplights, a set of train tracks that split the town down the middle, and farmland on all sides. There was a booster club, a Legion club, an Eagles club, and even a country club. So, yeah, it was happening.

After school, all I did was play with my friends. We would pull into the driveway and I would go right next door, knock, and hang out with my friend Anna until dinnertime. My mom and dad didn't have to organize playdates, or screen parents before granting access, or worry that a kid didn't have her shots. It was just "Go play." Can you imagine? Now parents ask for a dossier, SAT scores, and a background check on any family they might consider trusting their kid with.

My dad sold used cars at Dewey Hensley Motor, and my mom was a revered school teacher. I have a younger brother, Matthew, and a baby sister, Megan. We didn't go on fancy vacations or have expensive things, but I wanted for nothing.

We lived "in town" most of my life, but from ages eight to twelve, I lived on our family farm after my grandparents died and left it to us. My dad is a salesman, *not* a farmer, so when he tried to raise pigs, it was literally a shit show. My mother was forced to move from her beautiful house, which they'd built from the ground up, into a drafty farmhouse full of mice. She might not have chosen farm life, but it was heaven for an imaginative little tomboy of a kid with too much energy. I'd walk to the creek (crick) and fish for catfish, camp out in a barn or the hay loft, and spend endless hours making tree forts. I helped the vet birth pigs, and I even tried to raise a runt myself, but it died when I decided to keep it warm by putting it too close to the Earth Stove and then forgot about it while I was watching *ThunderCats*. I had a thousand cats, three dogs, six pigs, and one boar named Boris. One time the pigs were mating, and, horrified, I asked my dad, "What are they doing?!" He replied, "They're makin' bacon." Gross.

I'm part of a good-'n'-horny Catholic family hailing from western Nebraska. I have at least fifty-five first cousins, and it's anybody's guess how many second cousins. When my mom's side of the family has a reunion, they have to take an aerial photo, and they give us different colored T-shirts so you know which branch of the family tree you belong to. That's what they tell us anyway. I secretly think it's so no one closer than second cousins make out after a boozy barn dance.

We're a loud family. An open family. A call-it-like-you-see-it family. They let me be me, and thank God, because I could be a lot. There was always noise in our house when I was growing up. Good noise, like my friends Brandy and Kevin stopping by to raid the fridge while my mom was yelling up to my dad to put burgers on the grill. My parents insisted we eat meals together and talk to one another. No one had a TV in their room. We razzed each other about hairstyles and obnoxious eating habits. My mom set the tone for our family. She insisted on chaos, and I leaned into that hard. Chaos was all she knew because she is from a huge family. My grandmother Theresa had thirteen kids. She had seven, then none for five years, and then had six more!

All of them were born smart-asses, but number 13, Susie, was born with Down syndrome. She was a great source of love, laughter, and a sense of lightheartedness. Every family member showered her with love and presents, which included her favorites: gum, ham and cheese sandwiches, and anything with Hulk Hogan printed on the front of it. She loved bright pink tracksuits and animal prints. She was happy to paint her nails, watch *Dallas*, and giggle with her whole body. She died five years ago, and at her funeral it was standing room only.

Then there's my dad's side of the family. It's just him and his sister, Lois, who has special needs. She can barely read, and she has a palsy and a speech impediment. And yet, with all of those challenges, Lois has held the same job for over thirty years at a college cafeteria, and she has dated her boyfriend Rick (also challenged) for nearly forty years. She has an active social life, which includes playing basketball and boccie ball in the Special Olympics. She calls me every week and sends me a birthday card with a five-dollar bill inside every year. There is no question that at several times in my life my aunt Lois had a better apartment, love life, and credit score than I ever did. She is a perfect human.

While my folks came from different family setups, they both had a great sense of humor. My dad taught me the gratification of telling a good joke—or at least telling a joke that gets a big reaction. He is the world's best storyteller. He's animated and has impeccable comic timing. There isn't a dirty joke he doesn't know. When I was in first grade, I was sent to the principal's office for repeating a joke I'd overheard my dad telling: "How does a chipmunk scratch his nuts?" Then he'd puff out his cheeks and scratch his face. I had no idea what was so funny, but it made my dad laugh to tears, so I made sure to tell it to my teacher, the teacher's aide, my bus driver, and the school nurse the next day when I went to school. I was in trouble, but I wasn't alone. Both my dad and I were grounded for a week. It was a valuable lesson in knowing your audience, for both of us.

Life wasn't all roses and sunshine, though.

I have a very strong memory from first grade. I was sitting with all of my friends at a reading table, and this one kid told me to look under the table, and then he showed me his testicles. Wait, yes, that's a strong memory, but that's not the one I wanted to tell you about. Anyway, my friends and I were all

27

sitting at the reading table, and the teacher gave out colored cards to signify which reading group you were going to be in. Most of my friends went to the Orange group, which I quickly figured out was the "best" reading group, and I was put in the Yellow, which was just one notch below. That would define my academic standing for the next three years: just one notch below. I had decent but not great grades, I scored average on tests, and my teachers didn't complain much. I was doing "just fine." But "just fine" felt terrible. I wanted to be the best. I was driven, but everything just felt hard. Does everybody have to read the same paragraph thirty times to understand it? What I came to learn was that if I wanted to stand out, I would have to work three times as hard and three times as long.

I was about nine when I really knew there was something off about the way I learned. I had a strangely exhaustive work ethic, so my mom and dad were proud of me, not for my decent grades, but because they would see me work for hours to get my homework done. No one else seemed concerned, but inside, I knew something wasn't right. I'd be sitting in class, and all of a sudden I'd "come to" and find that the class was nearly over. *Where did I go? What did the teacher say? How do I catch up? Did I just space out? What is space? Are aliens real? I like fishing. Hold on.* Anyway, I couldn't sit still, and if I wasn't talking in class, I was doodling or thinking about the riveting conclusion to last night's episode of *Murder, She Wrote.*

And then puberty hit, and things got even more difficult. I was in such pain—I just truly hated myself. I am filled with dread at the thought of my children ever feeling for one second the way I felt for about four years.

My parents were very loving and understanding about how school and puberty were kicking my ass. I was confused by girls. I was confused by boys. I rarely laughed, and the friends who stuck with me—*God love them*—found me difficult and exhausting. That's a tough reality. All I wanted was for people to like me. And I just tried too hard to get their approval. I was loud in public and couldn't keep quiet during assembly. I always needed attention. It was like I was a puppet and someone else had control of the strings. Turns out the puppeteer had ADHD, and I went undiagnosed until the ninth grade. (More on that later.)

Cue the bullies. Girl bullies are not the same as boy bullies. Girl bullies don't give you wedgies or push you in the hallway; they play a mental game. They are cunning, cruel, and creative. They mess with your self-esteem and prey on your insecurities. Plus, I was fun to pick on because I was reactionary and impulsive and a super easy target. I had a mullet with a perm, so there was that. My mom and dad both played very important roles in my learning to cope with assholes.

My mom was a former high school special-ed teacher, and she taught a young gal named Jasmine, who was the youngest of six. Their mother was in prison, so all the kids lived with their dad. There is no reason to mince words here. The whole family was mean and loved to fight. Jasmine was no victim. She was tall, square-shouldered, and walked like a linebacker. Rumor had it that Jasmine was sick and tired of getting kicked around by her dad, so she punched him in the side of the head and blinded him in one eye.

Jasmine absolutely loved my mother, probably because my mom was sympathetic. She saw what was going on behind

29

people's behavior. She would tell me, "Not everybody in this world is dealt a fair hand." And my mom adored Jasmine. Years later, when my mom found out that the bullying toward me was starting to get physical, she talked to Jasmine because it was Jasmine's crew that was giving me hell. Out of nowhere the bullying stopped. At the time, I thought this was clearly a sign that Jasmine wanted to be my best friend, so when I saw her I chirped, "Hi, Jasmine!" and without hesitation she looked at me and said, "F*ck off." I smile just thinking about it.

It was about this time I had a very important conversation with my dad that deserves a spot on the highlight reel of solid midwestern parenting. One afternoon after school, I was outside crying about all the stupid things I had said and done that day. My dad came and sat next to me. I settled down a little because I knew he would say the perfect thing to make me feel better. He led with "Kristin, every dog has their day." *What?! Was he calling me a dog?* I sobbed harder. He continued. "Shit. I'm not doing this right. Okay. Deep breath. Kristin," he said with heavy resolve in his voice, "sometimes you just gotta say *f*ck it.*" I'd never heard my dad say that word before. It was wonderful.

He went on to tell me that if those assholes didn't like me for me, then they could go piss up a rope. It might be lonely at first, but eventually others would figure out that I was worth knowing. He said I was a bright shining light, that I was beautiful, and that my time would come. And I believed him. So, from then on, when I went to school and girls would mess with me, I just said "Ef it." (Ya know, to avoid the principal's office.) My new attitude made it possible for me to not take myself so seriously. I started to joke about myself, my appearance, my sweet dance moves. All of a sudden, humor became my weapon of choice. After that, my life and friendships changed, and I laughed all the time, mostly at myself but also out of joy. Laughing is the ultimate "f*ck you."

Things got better for me. Much better. In fact, here's something you don't hear people say very often: I liked high school. Loved it, actually. It wasn't perfect, but anything was better than middle school. After a few visits to a doc, I was taking a heavy dose of Ritalin every day. Ritalin wasn't a cure-all by any means, but it helped me focus and it calmed me socially. It also gave me terrible anxiety and insomnia, because nothing's free, but it did help me read a book cover to cover for the first time ever, and after busting my ass for years, I finally ended up in the Orange classes. Turns out I was pretty smart after all. Insert a big fat "I told you so" here.

By the end of high school, I was popular-ish. I was in every club and president of most of them. I loved theater and choir, played a mean clarinet in the band, played volleyball, and was a cheerleader. I loved speech team, the musical, and yes, at one point I was in Clown Troupe. My friend Lynn and I would dress up and drive to the Grand Island Conestoga Mall and just walk around. As clowns. For fun. On a Friday night. Shocker, but I did not have a lot of boyfriends, though I did have some crippling crushes that left their mark. If everything I just wrote doesn't indicate to you that I was a giant virgin upon graduation, then I am telling you now.

But I had friends. Real friends. Friends I cherish today, especially my girlfriends. They loved me the way I was, which felt amazing. The lot of us would laugh over the smallest, stupidest things with our heads back and mouths open. We would blast Nirvana or Beastie Boys and go cruising Main Street. If you aren't familiar with cruising, it's where you pack a bunch of people into your oversize Buick and drive from Pump & Pantry half a mile down to Gas-N-Shop and then turn around. Basically, it's a road trip in circles. You will put hundreds of miles on your car without going anywhere.

After I graduated high school, I went on to the University of Nebraska. My parents followed me—but not intentionally. My dad changed careers, so they moved to Lincoln during my sophomore year. My memories of Central are stored in a time capsule because once my parents moved away, I rarely had the opportunity to go back. I have a deep love for the Midwest and the people there. In some ways it's because I knew, once I left, I would never live there again—but damn if it's not always with me.

JEN

I don't think you can really say I'm from the "city"—it just felt that way to Kristin because her town only had those three stoplights. My hometown is Bellevue, which is roughly twenty times the size of where Kristin grew up. But that still isn't huge. Bellevue was founded in the 1830s, evidently as a fur trading post on the Missouri River. I'll let you insert your own beaver hunting joke here. The biggest things our town had going for it by the time I arrived were Offutt Air Force Base and a really great hot dog place with Skee-Ball, an arcade, and eventually waterslides. We also had a TG&Y, a mean rec center, and an epic sledding hill until it was leveled to build a Shopko and an Old Country Buffet.

There was the river on the east side of town, cornfields to the south and west, and the stockyards of South Omaha on the north side. For those of you who didn't have your senior prom at the stockyard exchange building, that's where ranchers from all over would go to trade livestock. There is a saying in the Midwest that livestock smells like money. The stockyards aren't operational anymore—I'm sure it's all done online—but neither are my olfactory glands since driving anywhere near there meant driving directly into that "money" smell, which explains why my perfume application is consistently at "saloon madam" level.

Now I have to admit, I wasn't born in Nebraska, though I do consider it my home. As anyone who is military will explain, you move around a lot. I was born at Walter Reed Army Medical Center in DC, lived in Falls Church, Virginia, and then landed in Nebraska for kindergarten. My brother was born in Japan, and we also lived in Illinois. When you're military, you either pick where you're from or just call the place you lived the longest your hometown.

There were two big reasons to go on base: the bowling alley and the commissary. My dad had the pleasure of taking us to the bowling alley pretty regularly, and my mother had the "pleasure" of taking us to the commissary every payday. The bowling alley was two basements below an airplane hangar and served beer. The commissary on payday was two levels below hell and sold beer. At the bowling alley, I mastered the only sports I am, to this day, any good at: those you can do while drinking. At the commissary, I learned you need to get there early, bring two carts, be prepared to stand in a checkout line that begins at the rear of the building, and of course, keep your hands out of the bags until you get home.

That said, I was always really proud of my dad, grandfather, and uncles for serving in the military. I loved when they dressed up in their class A's, and I loved going to base with them. We'd drive past the rows of stately brick homes occupied by the highest-ranking officers, past the missiles, past the landing bombers, past the art shop that my grandpa had helped open, past the temporary housing, and past the officer's club, knowing it was pretty cool to be a part of an American institution. I'd giggle when my relatives were saluted once we were on the base. They weren't getting that sort of attention at home, I can promise you.

My childhood wasn't all bad and wasn't all good; hey, neither was I. But I leaned into the fun of things, the laughter, the magic stuff, the mystical stuff, the stuff that could take you away, versus the stuff that kept you submerged in your own and other people's crap. One of the tough things about growing up near a military base is that your friends move away all the time. But I was lucky to have my family all living relatively close. I always had someone's house to go to when ours was empty or when people were tired of me. Nowadays, I worry about living so far from biological family. What will my kids do when they need to go to Grandpa's and build a mini stage to perform Shakespeare or want to pick tomatoes?

I always had my grandparents, aunts and uncles, and my cousin, and now that I know how terrible it is to raise kids and not have family nearby, I understand how much of a blessing that was. I was also lucky to have my brother.

My brother is responsible for keeping me alive for much of my life—and also responsible for dressing me in a wizard costume, tying me to a chair, and throwing me down the basement steps when I was nine. He's your typical older brother. Always showing off how great he is and beating me at Monopoly. Not only did he get the genes for good teeth, he's great at math and English. That's some bullshit, right? He has a BS in math, an electrical engineering degree, and an MBA, and he's getting another master's degree. Greedy. In our twenties, while I was at the bars, he kept himself busy teaching adults math in a GED class—and he's just generally nice to boot. My poor mom has to act like she loves us equally or I have a total meltdown, but trust me, I know who the favorite is. And I get it. My brother's a dream.

Sorry, Kristin, and every other friend I've ever had, but my brother has always been my best friend. I feel like we are twins born two years, four months, and sixteen days apart. We have the same ideas about stuff, can predict what the other will say, laugh at the same dark jokes, and have a genuine respect for one another. That's why, when I used ice and a quilting needle to pierce his ear to go with his sweet 90s mullet, we took equal punishment when my mom went bananas. I didn't get her anger at the time, but now that I'm a germaphobe and have grown ears in my own womb, I know I would not handle a DIY piercing well either. It's one step above a prison tattoo.

While we're on the subject of unauthorized pierced ears, my grandmother would frequently take me to the Southroads Mall, to Claire's, and get my ears pierced along with hers. You read that right: frequently. My grandmother Mimi was also like my twin, but born fifty-four years, one month, and three days earlier. She shared my love of jewelry. (I don't need lots of *fancy* jewelry; I just need lots of jewelry in general.) We had the same sense of style: I favored grandma style, she preferred teeny-bopper, and we met in the middle.

To say I was close to her and my grandfather Pappy would be an understatement. I drove to their house every morning in high school to drop my dog, Eric, at their house. Eric was old, and I was worried about him during the day. I'd drop him inside and have the most delicious fried eggs with Pappy every morning. We'd talk about the news, what was going on in school, or who was the latest victim of the violent Amazon crested parrot he bought at a discount store. If you've never seen a poodle and a Siberian husky run from a waddling parrot, you've never met Jose. Oh, and they also had a monkey named Tammy. Is it weird that two of my closest friends were my grandparents? Maybe, but if you had met Mimi and Pappy, you would want to be best friends with them too.

Until I was about eight, Mimi and Pappy lived in this tiny, terrible town in Oklahoma called Muskogee. My grandparents purchased an enormous house there, with maid's buzzers, dressing rooms, and chandeliers in the bathrooms, for about $20,000. There's never been a better house for visiting your grandparents—or sustaining lasting physical injuries. My brother cut his hand on the rusty swing set and still has a scar to this day. At age one, I fell, while in my walker, all the way down the basement steps, and I'm terrible at home organization to this day. Their giant three-level house was filled with sixty years of stuff they had collected and thrifted. The property was home to pipe organs, old cars, a four-foot fist shaped out of wire, laundry chutes, dumbwaiters, and I think lots of ghosts. For my brother and me, my grandparents' home provided endless entertainment, and a specific fear of a deceased dog groomer named Kenneth, who was rumored to haunt the place.

Last, but not least, I had parents. Duh. This one is tough for me right now because my dad passed away this past year, and I'm really missing him. It feels like a piece of my heart is in the next room, and I can't open the door to get it back.

My parents met during a tornado, in the tornado shelter of a trailer park, which pretty much set the tone for the fifteen years of their marriage. I was eight when my parents' marriage came apart at the seams. This happened to be the time in my life when I was just starting to love getting a laugh. Make of that what you may. My mom got a funky haircut and started dressing very *Miami Vice*, and my dad went middle-age crazy. They ended up getting divorced just before I became a teenager, which, no matter how hard everyone tried to make it easy, was crappy. I didn't really care if they were happy in their relationship. I just wanted us all to go out for pizza and get goodnight kisses from both of them. We felt the financial strain of their split, the exhaustion and sadness they both experienced, and on some level I got it, but when I was a kid, all I wanted to worry about was blue mascara and if Kirk Cameron would ever love me. Now that I'm an adult and I see how hard adulting is, my heart breaks a little for both of them. I know it's not what they planned for themselves or us.

As much as divorce sucks, I will say, if you ever want to see a woman go into full-on beast mode, give her two kids to raise by herself and tell her she can't do it. Postdivorce, my mom, who had only graduated high school and had not had a job outside the home in twenty years, put herself through medical school, became a physician's assistant, and could leap tall buildings in a single bound. Don't mess with a single mom. I thought she was Wonder Woman. She would fall asleep studying at the table. If I could take her mind off how hard things were, even for a second, I felt like a million bucks, so I'd try to make her laugh. Frankly, she probably wasn't in the mood for my act most of the time. But I was like, *Well, all right, I may not be perfect, but I can make some good jokes.*

Now, when I need to motivate myself, I think of my mom. She mommed *very* hard. Sometimes when I'm really tired, I'll think, *Hey self, you didn't work full-time, go to school full-time, and raise two angry prepubescents full-time today, so maybe you could fold that laundry.* And it works.

I think all the difficulties my mom faced getting her education later in life explains why she was so focused on my brother and me getting good grades and going to college. Both of my parents have master's degrees, and again, my brother is a show-off. Me? I graduated from college with a four-year degree in five and a half years.

As much as I felt loved, I don't think it would have surprised anyone if I didn't amount to much. That just wasn't always the expectation at that time in Bellevue. Not only was it not uncommon not to graduate from high school, I was at no point an exceptional student. Every teacher from elementary school on said the same thing to my parents at conferences: "She's a delight and she tries hard, but she cannot stop talking." (This is also what my husband might say about our romantic life.) One day, my fourth grade teacher took me out into the hallway and with a big grin told me, "Congratulations! You've tested as gifted and are eligible for some advanced studies!" It is possible the tests might not have been accurate. I did not know what her words meant. My husband teases me, "Oh, I'm sure you were in special classes, but I'm not sure if they were because you were gifted." When I see my old report cards, I think he maaaaay be on to something.

I did have some friends I wasn't related to. I met one of my first besties in seventh grade. Her name was Mandy, named after the Barry Manilow song. How great is that? To this day, she might know me better than anyone. We spent so much time together, hanging during the day and then sleeping over at each other's house. We would lie on her waterbed talking about boys, writing the names of the ones we loved on her waterbed mattress (yes, the part that can pop if you write on it with a pen—or so I hear), learning the words to our favorite Chicago and Air Supply songs. (Listen, we weren't friends because we were on the cutting edge of musical trends.) We were both short and skinny with snaggleteeth and a love of laughing. We can still make each other laugh like maniacs.

Like Kristin, I loved high school. Nobody was home at my house, so I did all the clubs—volunteering, speech, theater. I felt at home at school. I got there at 7:00 a.m. for dance practice and stayed until 10:00 p.m. for theater practice. And I still found time to get into trouble. I can sign my mother's name better than she can, so I would occasionally leave during the day. (Sorry, Mom.) There are a hundred reasons why skipping school is bad, and I did it for all of them. (Sorry, me.) Sure, there were shitty things about high school, largely my bad choices, but I loved it. I didn't hang with the cool kids, but I knew them. I got voted "Friendliest" and "Worst Driver." The driving thing was accurate. The "friendly" part must be because I've always been aware that everyone is dealing with something, with themselves or their family, and making other people smile always made me feel better about my things. My family taught me to do that. I tried to be nice at least, and funny at best. I'd like to say that's why I got multiple perms, but I think those may have just been bad choices. I can get into the sad stuff real quick, but I prefer to laugh about it all. When one bad thing happens, sure, I'm irritated and swearing. Two bad things and I'm raising my eyebrows and waiting for that third, comic beat to complete my story—that final "Are you kidding me?" to get me to laugh about the ludicrousness of it all. And by "all" I mean "life," that beautiful, beautiful bitch. I may not be Wonder Woman, but I make moms laugh for a living these days, and that feels good.

I BODY AFTER BABY SO HARD

Every woman has something about her body she would like to change. Jen's got a saber tooth. Kristin has bird-of-prey feet. You've got a little something, but you learn to live with it . . . and then you have a baby and your insecurity gets magnified a thousand-fold because you have this brand-new body you didn't order. You spend your teen years and your twenties dealing with what God gave you. Then you gotta spend the rest of your life dealing with what a pregnancy gave you. Once you've had a baby in your belly, weird excess skin will be the least of your problems. Your mental state is never the same. Your whole outside is never the same. Quite frankly, your actual hole is never the same either.

The battle is real. Women just tear themselves apart. Always have. Cavewomen were probably in their caves thinking, *If I*

could just get someone to eat this part of my stomach . . . We can understand that desire to just go into a plastic surgeon and say, "Take it all away." Sometimes, when we get together, we talk about all the plastic surgery we're going to get, like the thing where they do lipo on your stomach and your thighs and your butt and then put it in your boobs (that's what upcycling is, right?). We've got about twenty pounds between us that we'd love to leave in the rearview mirror—but not so much that we would stop eating pasta.

We did a video on swimsuits, and getting our post-baby bodies into them. We thought this was an issue specific to us, but after it received 100 million views, we realized that women of all ages, shapes, and sizes struggle with body image. Even the most beautiful women don't like themselves at times. How shitty is that? The upside is that knowing that even hourglass types feel a bit down about their bodies sometimes can make us compassionate toward other women and, more important, ourselves. Bottom line: we'd love a revenge body, but we'll take a "fuck it" attitude.

JEN

There is no justice in the world. You'd think that after bringing a whole new person onto the planet, you'd be rewarded with glowing skin and an amazing figure. But no. Things break down, starting at the bottom. Nothing works down there. I'm mangled. My vagina is like a basset hound with its head out the window, just flapping in the wind. I pee constantly. I pee when

I sneeze. I pee when I jump. I pee just before I sit on the toilet. And now I've started doing this thing where I think I'm done peeing on the toilet and I put my pants back on and go, "Oh, I'm actually still peeing." I'm like a guinea pig. When they get excited or you scare them, they squeal and pee. I should just have pee pads on my seat in the car and on my sofa.

If I'm standing at a party, having drinks, I won't even know I have to pee, but then I'll laugh—"Ha!"—and I start to pee. *Ha, ha, ha.* So I'll do this *Riverdance* thing, and I think that's going to hold it in, but it doesn't, so I just casually dance off to the bathroom, shuffling and stomping my legs.

Someone told me you are supposed to stand with your legs crossed to make yourself look smaller. I do that, but not because I think I'll look thin. (It's not like anybody is going to say, "Oh, until she uncrossed her legs I really thought she was super skinny, but then she took a step and . . .") I do it because I have to pee all the time, and also I'm scared an important part is going to fall out.

I used to feel like my legs were my only good part, and now they're so weird. I remember looking at my mom's legs and thinking, *Oh good, I got my dad's legs.* And then, ten years ago, I woke up one day and I was wearing my mom's exact legs. I used to have defined calves and thighs, even if I never worked out. Now I feel like my legs look like kebabs from one of those Brazilian barbecue places, just soft rectangles stuck together.

Growing up, I had so many friends who hated their legs. Even though I was short, I never wanted long legs. I never wanted to have to be responsible for that much equipment. That's a lot to shave and, in my case, apply self-tanner to. Which I do not advise doing after you have had wine. I looked like Tigger throughout my late twenties.

I'm glad I don't have cankles, but I do have spider veins. I got those when I was, like, eight. (I've always been precocious.) And my feet are so big that I look like a capital "L."

I have these strange dark spots on my knees. Have you gotten those? I had no idea what they were for the longest time. I thought it might have been from getting frisky in the bedroom, but then I realized that passing out at 9:30 every night without touching your husband does not bruise your knees. It was mommy knees. You get them from crawling around all the time and having no time to moisturize. I also have mommy feet, which means I'm standing in uncomfortable shoes all day and have no time for pedicures. And I have mommy ass, which means I eat a lot of leftover chicken nuggets and don't have time for the gym.

I used to plan my wardrobe around my legs, which I would only cover if I had cut myself shaving, but now, after having kids, I'm covering myself up in ways that I never did before. My husband tells me, "Well, that's because you weren't a chubby kid. Chubby kids just get used to wearing cover-ups at the pool and that kind of thing."

He's right. I did ballet and dance, which kept me thin. I mean, in high school, I used to eat two lunches every day. I know. I think I'm an asshole now too. Then, when I stopped dancing and started having kids, I just gained weight. Suddenly, I've got the body of a five-foot, ten-inch woman crammed into five feet. If I eat what a third grader eats, I'll gain a pound a day. German heritage is bullshit.

Here's where I'm at: I could have a better body, but I'm fine with how it is right now. I never thought that I was going to be in any magazines. (Well, it's not ballgame on *House Beautiful*. I'm working a real strong Hollywood Regency vibe into my living room right now.)

I don't want you to think I'm some crazy actualized superwoman who is made up of impenetrable confidence. It's more like I just don't care. It's almost like I've given up. My husband has seen it all anyway. He's literally the only person I care about whether he finds me attractive or not, and he does. Look, I'm not going to look great in a swimsuit anyway, so I'm not going to knock myself out trying to consume nothing but kale smoothies. Oh, I know I don't look like J-Lo in a bikini. I look like J-Slow, because I'm not going to run and spill my beer.

The weight that I am now is the weight that my body wants to be. I could do almost anything and it wouldn't change that much. Like, I could tone up more, but I don't know how much weight I'd lose unless I dieted like a crazy person, and it's just not worth it to me. I am always going to look like I like cheese, *because I like cheese*, you guys.

Lately, because of all the great stuff that's been happening in our lives, we go in these meetings, and we have this running joke right before we walk in, saying to each other, "Is this where they tell us that we have to lose weight? Is this the one where they tell us, 'We just need you guys to firm up a little bit. You're a little *too* real, you know?'" But it hasn't happened yet, and thank God, because I don't know how much happier I would be if I reached my theoretical goal weight again anyway. Or even if I had the most perfect body. It's never been the thing

45

that I led with. I'm not convinced that way lies happiness. I'd way rather have someone tell me my son said please than my butt looks great in my jeans.

"Way rather" might be kind of strong, but you know what I mean.

I'm not saying bust a gut and eat whatever you want if it makes you happy. I don't want anyone to eat in lieu of real actual happiness the way I sometimes fill the void with buying stuff online, but hey, if you make like a really mean Danish and you've been to the doctor and she says you're healthy, go ahead and be a little bigger. Who cares?

This is going to sound like when someone says, "I don't even see race, man. I'm, like, color-blind," but I honestly don't even notice what other people look like that much. I'm oblivious. Over the course of my life, I've seen maybe five people and thought, *Oh, that's unfortunate*. Kristin notices everything, like an FBI agent—mostly the bad stuff about herself and the good stuff other people are working with—and her brain just works a lot faster than mine does. She'll say, "I ran into Sarah. She's about to pop!" I won't have even noticed she's pregnant. That kind of stuff just isn't on my radar. Got a weird mole? A little extra junk back there? A unibrow? It just doesn't register with me. If we ever run into each other on the beach, I hope you'll return the favor. I'll be the one in the muumuu having an awesome time.

I know what you're thinking, that I've got something figured out about how to be happy. Incorrect. I'm a work in progress in so many ways. The reality is, I never considered myself a looker or a hot babe—quite the opposite. Kristin can leave the house without makeup, wearing sweats, and still look terrific. If I do that, I look like a sun-damaged, prepubescent boy who buys jeans in the Husky section.

I like to dress up and I always have makeup on, so you might think that means I take pride in how I look. It's actually a couple of things, neither of which is pride. One is habit. My life began with freckles, which transitioned into teen acne, which then morphed into hormonal cystic acne in my twenties. I had a few good years post-Accutane, but then came pregnancy acne and melasma due to breastfeeding. To top it off, now I have age spots. I have run the life cycle of bad skin, and I have always hidden it under lots of makeup. And I'm going down doing so. I keep telling my husband I'm still waiting for my day skin-wise. If it means I have to get all kinds of surgery and fillers, I'm going to GD do it. I deserve it. I'll look weird but young. Oh, the other reason is that I like to do it—I think makeup is fun. I feel like I'm being nice to myself when I put it on. It's like playing to me. I like to put it on other people. I could spend hours in a cosmetic store. Why can't I feel this way about the gym?

Being smoking hot at some point in your life must be a blessing and a curse. On one hand, you were smoking hot; on the other hand, that's a lot to maintain. I don't really like how I look, and never have, so it's never been a source of happiness for me—or even unhappiness for that matter. Just acceptance. That being said, I work with what God gave me, but I don't take care of it that well. I should have been valuing this love machine more. I've been pretty rough on it. I just started eating healthy veggies and fruit (thank you, kids, and the pressure to set a positive example). I just started noticing the mental health benefits of walking daily (or twice a week, or whenever the stars align—don't judge me). I'm old enough, and fearful enough of the universe, that I just want to be healthy. I still don't think I'll be on the cover of *Lowrider* magazine, unless they're featuring people who have world-class antique cut glass collections, but happy and healthy is all I need at this point.

KRISTIN

Jen loves being a girl. I don't hate it—I just find the mainte-nance exhausting. I want to be super attractive and beautiful and do zero work to get there. Sitting in a salon, having my nails done, tweezing my eyebrows, watching what I eat, going to the gym, staying up on trends, ugh, *forget it*. I find zero joy in it. I hate the process but love the result. I want to magically wake up and find that, for no reason at all, I dropped fifteen pounds and have abs again. I want to look in the mirror and see no signs of age, or fatigue, or a slowly emerging silver hairline. I want both nipples to be even instead of looking like those jokey glasses with eyeballs on springs. Looking great is hard work, and I'm pooped.

In general, we ladies are hard on ourselves. It's not easy to look at your reflection, know that it could be better, and pull the trigger on a new dress anyway. I once read a story about a woman who tried to not look at her reflection for one year. She got rid of all of her mirrors, avoided them in stores, and wore only clothes she felt great in. She did her makeup without a mirror! (Let's be real: I do that too.) She reported that she felt more self-confident, empowered, and generally happier in her life. I haven't gone that far, but I get it. Sometimes there seems to be so much wrong that you come to a point where you think, *This is as good as it's gonna get, and I'm okay with that.*

I love that Jen cares what Brit thinks about how she looks. (I'll bet he loves it too.) My husband tells me all the time that he thinks I'm pretty or that I look great. Sometimes I believe him, and sometimes I think he just wants to get out the door so we aren't late for the game. Obviously, I care about my husband's feelings, but if we are being completely honest, I care less about what he thinks and care more about what strangers think. It feels good to walk in to a room like you still got it. That doesn't come easily these days after having kids. It's hard to figure out what the formula is to feel good in your skin, especially if there's lots more of it due to children ruining your stomach.

I don't really worry about my legs like Jen does, but I can give you a real specific road map about how I feel about my double chin. And I carry a razor in my bag because I've got a sweet mustache and a full beard. I do Botox between my eyes because I get these four lines that make it look like I have a vagina on my forehead. My vanity is tested to the max when it comes to Botox because I hate needles, but I hate those vagina lines worse.

Jen only cares if *she* likes what she's wearing. I envy her. Also, she will tell you otherwise, but the woman has a great bod. I've seen her a hundred times when basically the only things she's covered are her choo choo and her nipples. She looks great. She's got killer style, but she's not all caught up in it. And she enjoys makeup and clothes the same way a baker enjoys a new frosting tip.

I'm oddly shy about my body, which you might not guess from the way I try to carry myself on our videos. I put on a brave front. When we shot the swimming suits video, I literally told myself, *Just don't look down*. Body image is a tough thing. I've struggled with it for a long time.

The summer between fifth grade and sixth grade was when my boobs did not get the memo that they were supposed to arrive. Quite the opposite. I managed to contract viral pneumonia and landed a stay in the ICU for dehydration. I spent all summer recovering, watching soap operas, and desperately missing my friends. When I went back to school, everyone had grown fifteen inches and had boobs and, one could only assume, pubic hair. Not me. I was still as flat as a board, and the hair that should have grown between my legs ended up on my eyebrows (think Bert or Ernie). I also had a sizable case of ADHD, which reared its ugly head at the exact same time. I was short, flat, loud, hyper, and sporting a giant unibrow, while my friends all looked like gliding gazelles. I longed to have their bodies and not my own. Enter "poor body image" here.

By age fifteen, my body decided it was time to give me my period and stack the deck on body hair. I grew five inches my junior year, and by my senior year I was one of the taller girls in my class. I even grew two more inches in college. I was a late bloomer.

I like to say I was in an awkward phase until age twenty-eight. By then, I had started to figure out who I was. I was a bartender for a very long time, and I remember one night two women walked into the chichi bar I was working at in Santa Monica. They were wearing very similar outfits, short skirt, low-cut top, all black. They had basically the same shape body, yet one chick looked really attractive and the other girl looked . . . a little desperate. *Why?* I wondered. I realized it was their energy. The one gal who looked like a million bucks felt comfortable in her skin and comfortable with herself. That outfit was her style. Meanwhile, the other gal was clearly trying to get attention but was not okay with herself. I realized at that moment that I am the most attractive, the sexiest, when I am comfortable. For me, a booby top and stilettos ain't gonna fly, but if that is what makes you feel good, then lean in, girl. Once I realized that it's not how you look, it's how you feel, man did it help me. I started to think about that in relation to my life and who I spent my time with, where I lived, and how I lived, and by thirty I had a much better understanding of myself. Thirty is a fantastic age. It's the dawn of the "I don't give a damn" stage, which is also very, very sexy.

I waited and waited for boobs, but they never came in. I'm not saying, "Oh, they were small for my frame." They were *invisible*. They did not exist. To look like I had any boobs at all, I had to stay dangerously thin. That was super hard and not worth the hassle, so I bought a pair. Yes, I got my boobs done. Say what you want about plastic surgery, it was a great decision for me. You might think I'd be showing those puppies off the way marathoners wear their "finisher" medals everywhere, but I wore one booby shirt and I said, "Nope. I don't like this." I'm back to concert tees and boots. Then nursing ruined my beautiful fake boobs. Now they look real, which sucks because I didn't pay for real. I paid for real perky.

I've been the same weight for four and a half years. Now the only thing that's skinny about me is my legs and my ankles. I have what some might refer to as a "mom bod." It's hard to always accept my new body because I just want to wear a tighter T-shirt and jeans, but I've got this middle. Clearly, my midsection is the head of operations and decided it would be more efficient to keep all of my fat centrally located rather than divvy it out to all areas. I like to play a game called "pregnant or period" every morning. It's hard to dress cute with a thick middle. You look like a football wearing clothes.

My stomach really bothers me sometimes. I was hanging out at Jen's house a couple of months ago, and I told her I wanted to get a tummy tuck. She was like, "I don't know what you're talking about. What's going on down there that you think is so bad?" So I told her, "I'm going to finally show you, Jen. I'm going to finally show you." I steeled myself, got hold of my shirt, and slowly pulled it up. I was grabbing the pudge and stuffing the skin back into my jeans like it was a tube of Pillsbury crescent rolls that I was trying to shove back in the can. I felt so ashamed. I looked at Jen, and she was incredulous. She said, "That!? That's what I have!" And she lifted up her shirt and said, "Am I supposed to be upset about this? That's what everybody has. Should I be going to get a tummy tuck too?"

I looked at her and thought, *Huh. She's so skinny, but she kind of does have a little bit of stuff.* Then it hit me that *everybody* kind of has a little bit of stuff. And if you don't have a little bit of stuff, I'm sure you have something else that you're masking or hiding or ashamed of.

That's why I have to hand it to my sister.

Here's what I will tell you about her. She's five feet ten, taller than me, so we're bigger people to begin with. She's a little thick too. We went to the beach last summer, and you know that initial feeling of taking off your swim cover-up that feels so creepy? It's like you're basically getting naked in front of strangers because you kind of are. It makes everybody feel weird. There is a moment when you think, *Can everyone see my cellulite?* Or you notice a huge strip of hair that never made it close to a razor. Or you wonder, *Are my spider veins as bright as Christmas lights?* I get wrapped up in those moments sometimes, and then I stop enjoying myself. Meanwhile, Megan was the first one in the water, laughing and splashing like a midwestern mermaid. I thought, *Damn, she's got a lot of confidence, and she's wearing it.* She had so much joy.

I realized then that joy is so sexy. But it ain't easy. Being self-conscious is second nature. Or maybe first nature. I still struggle sometimes, but then I tell myself, *You know what? My friend Brandy who died of cancer would have given anything to trade places with me right now. And she'd kick my ass for wasting time worrying about it.* I have a healthy body and I'm criticizing myself because, what, I have a little bit of cheese on my thighs? Sometimes you have to gut-check yourself. Yup, I have a gut. Check.

I try. But it's hard because I do let other people's opinions affect me. I care about what they think. Like my mom.

My mom likes to tell dirty jokes. (I get that from her.) She loves to buy shoes. (I get that from her.) And she's incredibly hard on herself about her weight. (I get that from her.) I get a few things from my father too: I'm a great storyteller, I'm a loud laugher, and I have a significant midsection.

My mother has always been thin, and she has always been obsessed with food. She's a tough one to figure out. She eats

53

like a bird and then posts food porn on Facebook daily. Every time she shares something, it's like a recipe for a seven-layer mac-and-cheese with a double fudge cake chaser. The videos are set to erotic music, and they serve the food real slow. My husband and I have a running joke that right before she takes a bite of something delicious, she always says, "I *never* do this . . ." My mom walks every day, and she also spends time at the gym four days a week working out in the swimming pool because she's newly retired and has a pretty gnarly back injury. My point is that she has the time and the desire to focus on herself, and I don't. Or I choose not to. My mom looks fantastic at sixty-eight, and it's because she works at it. She's active and fun, but she doesn't really understand the struggle of being overweight. My mom put on some weight when I was eight. I don't remember it—she just talked about it incessantly. She joined Weight Watchers, and from that point on we never had dessert again. She makes no apologies for staying fit. She wants to be around for the grandkids as long as she can, and she isn't trying to chase her youth. She'll say things like "I love being an active senior." She wants to live a long and healthy life. Ain't nothin' wrong with that. With that being said . . . it can be difficult at times when she comes to visit and wants to "offer a suggestion" about how I can improve my "crazy lifestyle." It's better if you reread that sentence with a real thick midwestern accent.

Over the last couple of years with #IMOMSOHARD, my mom has shifted in ways that are pretty incredible. At first, my brutal honesty (especially in the live show) made her uncomfortable because she's my mom and I was talking about married sex or being proud of my giant vagina. Ya know, things moms shudder at. But now, she's gotten to a place where she is completely supportive of me and believes in the community we are trying to build. She says things like "I never had anyone to tell how I really felt when I was a young mother. Can I have seventeen free tickets for your cousins in Denver?"

Jen always reminds me that I'm not allowed to say things about myself that I wouldn't let someone else say about her. If someone called Jen fat, I'd turn into the Hulk and roundhouse-kick them in the head. She's right. I have to learn not to be so mean to myself: I have a little girl with big ears.

There was one day a few weeks ago when I was looking in the mirror, and I said, "Man, I've gotten so fat." Eleanor was right behind me and heard every word. Her face. It looked like I'd hurt *her* feelings when I said that. I got so mad at myself. She thinks I'm so perfect, and I'd just told her I'm not, so in some weird way it was like I was telling her she's not. It hit me like a ton of bricks, and I was like, *That's it. This cycle stops with me.*

My daughter is strong like a little softball player. She loves karate and she's very athletic, but a few weeks ago, another kid in her school told her that she had big legs. The little girl compared her legs to Eleanor's, and this girl was very, very teeny. Eleanor came home and asked me, "Mommy, why do my legs look different than the other girl's legs?" I just want to be clear that Eleanor is extremely normal—like beautifully, perfectly, heartbreakingly normal—but this other girl was super petite. She looked like a keychain. Also, they're five, for the love of God. I had a million emotions at once, but I don't like to cry. I was trying so hard to keep it together, so I managed to say, "Your legs make you fast and strong like a superhero, and you're perfect." Then I went into the bedroom and I sobbed.

When Jen heard about it, she started taking out her hoop earrings and threatened to go to the school with brass knuckles, but I was like, "Down, girl. It's a five-year-old. You'll lose."

So now I say stuff like "I feel really strong." I don't talk about skinny or fat. Instead, I say, "Mommy went to a spin class today, and she wasn't terrible." I tell Eleanor how powerful she is. How healthy she is. She is probably so tired of it, but I constantly look at her and lay it on thick. "Eleanor, your eyes are magical." "Eleanor, you are literally the best artist on planet Earth." Or "Eleanor, you are so cute I could just cry." (Then she rolls her eyes.) I want her to complain about it someday: "Gather around, girls. My mom is the *worst*. All she did was constantly remind me that I'm amazing and magical, and now I have so much confidence I don't know what to do with it." Then I'll let one of her girlfriends smack her.

My goal is to get reports from her school that Eleanor is *too* confident. Or that she thinks too much of herself, that she thinks she is the bomb diggity. I will deal with those issues when they come because the world will work against her, and she needs as much ammo as she can get going in. I want her to feel like she is fucking fierce, like she rules the goddamn world. (She *will* get that from me.)

I BUST MY ASS SO HARD

It's no secret. We moms are under a lot of pressure. Birth-day parties are now extravaganzas. Holiday cards are historical markers of our failings. The amount of yelling we do is directly proportional to the odds our children will go to prison for a white-collar crime. You know, the basics.

We will never stop trying. No matter how much we tell ourselves to take the pressure off, we will automatically put the pressure back on because, at the core of it, our efforts are equated with how much we love those little people. They will know we love them. (And they will love us back, damn it.)

God forbid we ever feel "enough," right? The moment we relax, we think, *What else should I be doing right now?* We feel guilt when we take care of ourselves. We neglect our own sleep and health for the sake of others, and undoubtedly someone will still tell us that so-and-so's mom is nicer. Great. Send her over. We could use the help.

It's never easy to ask for help, not because we are stubborn, but because we assume every mom is busy, so why should we add to her already-full plate? Here's an idea: as a collective, how about we make an effort to *offer* help to one another? "I'll bring a plate of my famous sugar cookies to the party." "I know you can't go to the school recital, so I'll take lots of video." "You've been with the kids all day. Can't you sneak away and have a glass of wine with me in your driveway?"

Vulnerability is the truest measure of courage. To say to someone, "I don't know what I'm doing and I need help," is not weak; it's brave. By the way, *we don't know WTF we're doing.* Are we the bravest people in the world? Who cares? Just please, someone show us how to get the mold out of sippy cup straws.

Somehow, when we weren't looking, an insidious little worm of an idea began spreading through parents' minds, like lice through a kindergarten class. While we were checking our Instagram accounts and happily scrolling through Pinterest, this little worm started to whisper in our ears that to be considered a good mom, everything has to be homemade, it has to be the best, and it has to be photographed within an inch of its life, using the right filters to showcase how incredibly charming and adorable your children are. Heaven forbid we just go to Target and buy some stuff.

We moms are knocking ourselves out, trying to knock it out of the park. It's like social media is the metaphorical grumpy coach telling us that every time we step up to the plate, it's got to be a grand slam or it doesn't count. We're here to tell you: just get on base. Or just bring the cooler of beer. Either way, you're winning in our book.

Old-school moms get it. They think we're *crazy* for doing everything ourselves when we don't have to. We're not pioneers, for crying out loud. We have microwaves. And dishwashers. Recently, Kristin asked her mom for her homemade cinnamon roll recipe, and her mom was like, "For goodness sake, just buy them. They're a pain in the ass to make." Jen's mom never felt pressure to be Pinterested and perfect. She knew that no one was going to call CPS if Jen ate a little laundry detergent. And Jen turned out just fine. Sure, she might have a light-to-medium obsession with serial killers, but at least she *isn't* a serial killer.

Here's what we've learned from a few years of occasionally succumbing to the siren song of looking good on social media. No matter how many likes you get, no one is going to give you the World's Best Mom trophy. As long as your kids are fed, safe, and happy sometimes, you're winning. Doing things perfectly takes away from what your kids *actually* need—a happy mom. Because when you're making 12 million tissue paper flowers for the end-of-year class performance, there is so much else you are not doing. Like hair brushing. Teeth brushing. Pants putting on. Plus the stuff you have to do to take care of your kids.

Are you a magician? Are you Gandalf? No! You're just a woman. Be okay with average. Be a seven. It's a lucky number.

JEN

Pinterest was not created by a mother. It was created by a motherf*cker.

As much as I'd like to tell you that I float like Beyoncé above it all, I have definitely gotten the Pinterest bug on occasion. I was once Pin-spired to make a life-size papier-mâché alligator for a friend's kids' Halloween party. Alligators are big, you guys. This was not some dinky Geico gecko. This was the Crocodile Dundee of fake gators. It was five feet long with individually hand-sculpted teeth and a custom paint job that would have made the dudes who trick out their lowriders jealous. And we didn't even *go* to that party. Another time, I made a dragon that had actual smoke coming out of its nose (no big deal, just some dry ice, ingenuity, and two and a half weeks of painstaking work) that was up for about sixty-seven minutes at an event. You know who noticed? Nobody. (Side note: Having an event? I will apparently make you any reptile or reptile-adjacent creature you desire.)

Maybe it's my reptilian brain, telling me to take care of my young because it feels that genetically encoded. My DNA tells me to hand-make bows at my own peril.

The Pinterest plague hits me especially hard because I like to have parties for people. I like to host because I want people to feel special, like somebody cared that they had a good day. So for my daughter's first birthday, I planned a tea party, just like every one-year-old who can't even hold a cup yet has always wanted. I handcrafted invitations, put them in the mail, and told everyone they had to wear tea party attire: boys formal, girls in spring dresses. I went out and bought dozens of vintage hats—top hats, garden party hats, church hats—for our guests on the off chance they didn't have their own tea party–appropriate headgear. Kristin put curls in her hair and everything. I sewed a really stinking cute skirt for Delilah out of tulle, which was like wrestling a fish, and made her a felt crown with ONE embroidered on it.

And friends, I decorated. I had paper balls everywhere. I hung lights, arranged flowers, and bought macaroons. Everything was white and wicker and just covered in bows. It was like I was gunning for the cover of *Martha Stewart Living: Toddler Tea Party Edition*. If I died in a train wreck, I wanted Delilah to see pictures of that day and think, *Damn, that woman loved me.*

Delilah was supposed to take a quick refreshing nap before the party started, so that she'd be at peak delight. I put her down and she screamed for a while, but I wasn't worried. I thought, *Poor thing. She's just excited and tired. I'll let her fuss it out.* After about ten minutes of baby rage, it got quiet, and I let myself feel smug, telling myself, *See, I knew that was all my girl needed. Let the #blessed-fest begin.*

But then something changed.

The quiet got eerie, like *The Conjuring* eerie.

All of a sudden, Delilah let out a monstrous scream. I ran into her bedroom. The moment I opened the door, I didn't even need to turn the light on to know what had happened. I just started shouting. People ran in—my brother, Kristin, my husband. Everyone stopped dead in their tracks. *Oh crap.* So much crap. My daughter had Picasso'd the entire area surrounding her crib and, for that matter, the entire area inside her crib and its contents—her body, her hair, her stuffed animals—with her shit. "Everywhere" does not begin to describe how pervasive the poop was. The dream party I had envisioned for months was now an episode of *Law & Order: Fecal Victims Unit*. Everyone was really quiet, and then Kristin turned to me and said, "Er, Jen, does this mean I can take off my hat?" No. No, it doesn't.

I finally let go of the breath I'd been holding since I got the idea for the party in the first place, and got to work scrubbing. And laughing. The party wasn't exactly what I had imagined. My Pinterest dreams had gone up in a glorious blaze of baby poo. Instead of the handmade wonderland and ball gown I'd imagined, Delilah wore a perfectly fine dress from Carter's, and the paper balls were being used as soccer balls about ten minutes in. At least the macaroons were good. Yeah, her dress was ruined, but we got some great pictures. In fact, the best family picture I've ever taken is one of our crew sitting in a spot that had been smeared in poop five minutes earlier. I still find poo on her crib sometimes. I know, super gross. Sue me.

I haven't learned my lesson, and I don't plan to. This year for Halloween, I'm making an octopus costume and a pony costume instead of folding laundry. Because I like to. But if you don't, just buy the damn costume. Do what makes you happy. Moms don't get away with that enough.

KRISTIN

Pinterest and I have a love-hate relationship. I love to hate it. I had one of my worst days as a mother because of Pinterest fooling me into believing in the importance of Teenage Mutant Ninja Turtle–shaped cake pops. I also hate cake pops. And baking is not my thing. It was Finn's third birthday, and somewhere along the way it was imprinted on me that the only way to show true love to your child is to bake homemade cake pops while working a full-time day job. Oh Pinterest, your pictures are so alluring, enticing, and full of unattainable expectations. It's like every guy I went for in my twenties. Fine, I'll try it. So I snorted a big line of Pinterest and made my way to Michaels craft store, another place I can't stand, and I bought everything on the list. Fondant? I don't even know how to say it much less use it or shape it or whatever. But I was determined, I have an advanced degree, and there is a tutorial for everything, so how hard could it be? Hard. Really, really hard. Five hours later, the kitchen was covered in frosting, the fondant looking like a wad of gum, and nothing resembled a TMNT. I had failed. Now my three-year-old son would never know I loved him.

My husband came home that night and found me coming down from my high. He let me cry and cry hard. Then we laughed even harder. I took a picture of the mess, sliding my right hand in to give the whole process the bird, and I shared it on my Facebook page. That picture had more likes than my wedding photo.

My new criteria for projects is this: Can I make this and not have a psychotic episode? Most of the time, the answer is "Nope!" so that's when I remind myself that sometimes you just have to throw cash at the problem. That is the whole reason those places like BounceU were invented. I show up and some stoned-looking seventeen-year-old in a polo shirt escorts my children from room to room while I eat pizza and slice the personalized (store-bought) cake? Do you take American Express?

Now, if I'm hosting a party at my house, instead of falling down into a Pinterest vortex—where I go hard, feel inadequate, and put in a good forty-eight hours of rage—I just go straight to Party City and buy everything on the clearance table for my kids' birthday parties: SpongeBob, the Minions, and some off-brand Anna and Elsa, so we can all live in creepy harmony. Anything as long as I don't have to poke lollipop sticks in individual balls of dough. All my kids really care about is frosting anyway, and Betty Crocker sells that in a can.

My biggest problem isn't Pinterest—it's pleasing. I just want everyone else to be happy. Okay, that doesn't sound so bad, but it is when I will chew off my own leg to make sure other people are having a good time—'cause that's what people find fun, right? Watching a grown woman gnaw on her femur? And then drive myself to the ER, 'cause "I got this. You guys have fun playing corn hole without me. There's Coke Zero in the fridge!" Let's be honest. A bad day for me is going to be even worse for my husband. I can't shoulder all that rage on my own. Shit's gonna roll downhill.

A lot of moms are like this, I think. We brave-face it. We spend all day killing ourselves to get our house together—or at least to the point where it looks like our kids are not feral—and then we open the door with a smile even though our mascara has run down to our chin from ugly crying at our failure to keep ourselves together. We say, "I'm so glad you're here" and "It wasn't any trouble at all." Who do we think we're fooling? We spent all day making the house smell like cinnamon and butter when it usually smells like cheese sticks and feet, and what we're really thinking is *Why the hell are you on time? Don't you know to come at least twenty minutes late?*

I'm like a golden retriever. Even if I feel sick, or if I feel hurt, I'm just like, *Nope, I'm okay*, because I want everybody to have fun. At a dinner party, I take the seat closest to the kitchen so I can dash in there any time anyone needs anything, even if all I've managed to eat all day is an olive that rolled on the floor that I couldn't bring myself to throw away because I'd shelled out for the marinated kind instead of the cheap ones that come in a can. I could have a broken hip and you're not going to know it because we moms just don't want to bring anybody else down.

This year, I went out with some girlfriends for my birthday to a funky little restaurant. We sat outside on a beautiful night and had beers and ordered some salty fried appetizers and a boatload of happy hour oysters. After about twenty minutes, my stomach did a flip turn. I had the cold sweats and I could feel my cheeks turn sepia, the barf-colored crayon. I was like, *What is happening?* And then very quickly it became very clear: *Ohhhhh, I'm going to throw up these oysters.* Or, um, something else these oysters. But my brain was like, *Kristin, this is a great time, so DO NOT say anything. Look at them. They're just laughing and kicking it, and they're here for YOU, so you just shut it.* Finally, one of my friends noticed that I was basically holding back barf with one hand and diarrhea with the other, and said, "Hey, Kristin, if you don't feel good, we can just call it." I was like, *Waaaaaah?*

But she was right. We've got to be okay just saying, "Hey guys, I don't feel well," and putting ourselves first.

As moms, we *never* put ourselves first, we don't even put ourselves second. We're down around number twenty-seven, along with shopping for a new area rug, finding a hairdresser who plays videos to distract your kid while she gets her hair cut, and figuring out what supplies your child needs for his unit on owls and butterflies.

Moms can't even take our own good advice and get our butts to the doctor regularly. Jen's dog goes to the vet more regularly than she goes to the doctor. It's hard to make that time for yourself, but you just gotta. If your kid has a recital, and that's the only time you can go in and get a mammogram, your kid is going to be okay. You need to go get that mammogram.

Besides, your kid won't even remember. When we did our summer tour, I was crushed 'cause I missed Finn's spring program. I gave Colin a five-minute lecture on how to record the whole thing. He knows what he is doing, most of the time. He's an intelligent adult. It is possible he did not need my instructions, but I really didn't want him to mess it up. I should have been relishing the joy that performing gives me, but instead I nearly gave myself an ulcer worrying about whether Finn would ever forgive me for missing his program. In the end, that kid barely noticed I was gone. He had like zero clue. I was way more upset about my missing it than he was.

Let me let you off the hook: the next time you eat discount seafood, your Aunt Kristin is giving you permission to call it a night and head back home. Your friends will still love you. No one is perfect. In fact, it is way more fun not to be. Besides, they don't want to have to pay the vomit fee to have an Uber steam cleaned. It's $250, BTW. Ooooof.

I BALL AND CHAIN SO HARD

Marriage is the hardest thing about parenting—and there are *a lot* of hard things about parenting.

Think of the most romantic date you have ever been on with your husband, partner, baby daddy, or whatever fits the bill. Think about the long lingering looks and leaning over the table to hold hands or smile softly over candlelight and perfectly prepared polenta. Now imagine that the bottom of the restaurant floor opens up, and all of a sudden you are both skydiving and your bodies are plummeting to the ground at warp speed. Common sense says to pull the cord, but you can't think straight because you've never done this before, so you look to him for help or to save you, and he is fully bawling. So you start to argue mid-fall, and then you fumble around and eventually find the rip cord, pull it just in the nick of time, and float to the ground with minor bumps and bruises and lots of resentment. This is what it's like when you add a baby to the mix. It's a free fall, but eventually you land and most of your injuries are emotional.

In the end, the most important thing is that you find yourself next to the best possible person for the job. And that is why we are both grateful for the men we married. We know we got good ones. Don't get us wrong—our husbands make us insane, but we have no intention of leaving them. We would never give them that freedom.

We like to think of our husbands as modern men. They don't come home and expect a hot dinner and a Scotch on the rocks to be waiting for them. They are knuckle-deep in kid shit just as much as we are, and they can even be pretty emotional when the occasion calls for it—like when they talk about sports.

Both Colin and Brit were football players in their younger days, and both love the game and everything surrounding it. But what they really love about sports is a good sports story.

Here's a typical exchange: "Hey, Brit. Did you hear the story about the running back who was drafted and he gave his . . . ," Colin chokes back tears, "his signing bonus to the lunch ladies . . ." Brit interrupts and continues the story, ". . . because his mom didn't have enough money when he was growing up, and the school lunch ladies would feed him when he was hungry? Yes. I read that." (Sniffles.) They both play off their weeping as a coughing fit.

It's that combination of masculinity and tenderness that makes our marriages work, especially now that we are going all out for #IMOMSOHARD. Both of our husbands did an absolute about-face in order to support the two of us as things started to heat up, and we know that took real strength. We would not be where we are today without them. And when we travel, they will remind us: "You don't know how hard it is to be home with the kids all day."

Blank stare.

Deep breath.

Grin.

Yes. Yes, we do.

KRISTIN

I wasn't sure if I would end up married with children. Neither was my mother.

I had no interest in being in a relationship in my twenties. I lived my twenties the way they were intended: full of shame and regret. I refer to that decade as my second adolescence. It was the first time I had lived away from home and was capable of making my own decisions. I made lots of decisions, bad ones that usually involved too many shots of tequila and a barback named Ryan. My twenties were awful and formative. I started to take note of what felt good and what felt like I was destroying my soul. Did I make mistakes? You bet. But I am who I am because of them. Also, I got rid of Ryan.

When I turned thirty, I dated the wrong guy for three years. I knew it was wrong after three months. When it ended, it was like someone had blown a hole through me. I had thought it would be easy since he wasn't right for me and I knew it. But it was *hard*. Luckily, Jen got me through that dark time, and I basically became a third wheel to her and her new boyfriend at the time. I dated Bri-Jen (Brit and Jen) for a long time. Brit always paid for my dinner, and Jen always put out. It worked out nicely.

Jen loves self-help, so she helped me work through a lot of pain. She talked about love languages and numerology, and then she made me a chart and had me write affirmations. It was like boot camp for the soul. I usually make fun of her about this stuff, but I was so broken that I welcomed the help. Jen worked her magic on me, and in time I healed up.

While I was working through that stuff, I taught English and drama at a continuation high school, which is essentially a high school designed for kids who were kicked out of public education. Most of my students were on probation or community service. I was hired to teach for one year as a long-term sub, and I stayed for seven. Before I became a mother, teaching was the most gratifying and rewarding experience I'd had in my life. My students were considered the "tough kids," but they were the only ones I wanted to teach. They had depth and grit. They were honest and hopeful and at times very difficult. I taught an improv-comedy class and was determined to have the comedy show in a proper theater and not in a cafe-torium. I heard that a new theater had just opened in Santa Monica called the Westside Comedy Theater, so I called and spoke to their artistic director. His name was Colin.

I had it all worked out in my head. I would walk into that theater, bat my eyelashes, and ask them to give me theater space for my "at-risk teens." What kind of monster would say no? But I was late for my appointment, and when I walked into the theater Colin was hanging theater lights and wearing a tool belt and a tight black T-shirt. He descended the ladder and smiled. His eyes sparkled when he spoke, and I got nervous and dorky. And I giggled. *I don't giggle.* Suddenly, I forgot how to bat my eyelashes and just started hard-blinking a bunch. I was a mess. It wasn't his good looks or his sexy tool belt that gave me butterflies—it was his warmth. It was palpable. He was charming and likable and funny. He was over six feet tall and had dark hair with, I was happy to see, a little salt and pepper. I knew he was younger than me, but I wasn't sure by how much. I prayed he was over thirty. He was. By one month.

Luckily, my very un-smooth moves worked, and Colin and the other owners of the theater agreed to put up the show at the Westside. Colin asked if he could coteach, and I said *Yes!* way too fast. Needless to say, I felt it was *very important* that Colin and I meet for as many lunches as possible to go over the program. I was doing it for the children, of course. Meanwhile, the second we would start lunch, in my head, we were on a date. I came on way too strong. I showed up at his theater "just to check out a show," I friended him on Facebook, and I cockblocked him from a girl he was clearly flirting with by saying mature things like "She looks like she has an STD." I knew I was doing it all wrong, but wrong felt right. I went with it.

Turns out, Colin and I work really well together. We taught fifteen challenging teenagers the joy of improv comedy, and we did it together. He is a very talented improviser and comedian. He was incredible with my students and coached improv in a way that made them feel brave. For example, one of my students, Antonio, was gay, very shy, and very into the Twilight series. When he started a scene and was clearly terrified, Colin jumped in and pretended to be Edward from Twilight, and then Antonio played Bella, and he just totally transformed. It was such a joy to see Antonio feel so confident. We worked so hard to build the kids up and prepare them for a live audience. Colin became a regular presence at the school. And soon, my students picked up on the fact that I had a major crush. Whenever Colin was scheduled to come to the school for rehearsal, I wore lipstick and a cute outfit. The kids were onto me: "Oh, look who did her hair. Is it because Colin is coming to the school today, Miss Hensley?" I'd snap back (tossing my admittedly voluminous hair), "Shut up, Chauncey. . . . Why? Did he say something?"

After six weeks of rehearsal, the show was a great success, and we decided to coteach another improv class right away. I loved being around Colin, but he was giving me zero signals that he was interested in me as more than a coworker. It was super frustrating and very confusing. I was throwing down my best game, and by thirty-four, I had *perfected* game. But he wouldn't make a move. Finally, I did something that would change the course of our relationship forever. I asked him to sub on my coed softball team. There was a lot to risk here. (1) We were undefeated, so if I brought a dud to the field I would be forever shunned by the softball community. (2) This was our first non-school-related activity. (3) My softball team brought me more joy than anything else. It was my turf, both literally and figuratively. And now I had invited Colin into my happy place. When he showed up to the field, it was like I could only walk on my tiptoes. Gross. And again with the giggling.

He played shortstop and I played first base, and every time he fired the ball at me I had a mini-orgasm. Gross. For me, if a guy can play softball and can build shit, that guy is getting to third base, no question. But still, Colin gave me no indication that he wanted to—for lack of a better word—round *my* bases. It was too much to handle. I was like, *What is wrong with this guy? We have so much fun together and he just played on my softball team and he can clearly see I have a nice ass. I'm a cool fun chick, so just love me, for Pete's sake!*

Finally, we had a couple of drinks at a bar (he had several), and he kissed me on our walk home. He spent the night . . . on my couch. He was hammered. He said he accidentally drank too much because he was nervous and had liked me for a very long time. The next morning, when I checked on him, he pulled me toward him and kissed me. And then we humped like a thousand times.

Jen knew something was up because it was radio silence on my end when Colin and I started dating. I was madly in love and spending all of my time with him. Jen and Brit had become so used to me being on dates with them that I'm sure they were confused when the host would seat them and there were only two chairs. Jen invited us over for New Year's. It was a big night for me. I really wanted her to like him and for Brit to give me the thumbs-up. I didn't need to worry. It ended up being the greatest New Year's ever. We played Running Charades, and Colin and I were on different teams. We were competitive and playful, and Jen adored him.

Three months after New Year's, Colin proposed at his theater during the high school comedy show while we were on stage together. He packed the house with friends and loved ones. I didn't see it coming at all, and during a game of freeze tag, Colin got down on one knee and was holding a ring. All I remember is that

I ugly-cried. Jen and Brit were there and took us for champagne afterward. Jen said it felt like being in the audience of *The Price Is Right* during the Showcase Showdown. It was epic. Then we left the next day for a friend's wedding. We were so overcome with newly engaged bliss that we pulled over and made passionate love in a Carrows parking lot in the front seat of my MINI Cooper. It was very classy. And very potent.

Did you know that if you have unprotected sex you can get knocked up? The fact that it happened in my MINI Cooper was mind-blowing. Were his sperm attached to a rocket? We told my mom (not where or how it happened, but that I was pregnant), and she celebrated like it was the fourth quarter of a playoff game and I had kicked a winning field goal. "Yes! We didn't know if it would ever happen. Thank the lord!" We told Colin's mother, a proper Southern Christian woman, and she was confused as to how a woman could get pregnant before her wedding. A few months later, I said "I do" in Palm Springs wearing an expandable dress. I looked like a fat country singer.

We did everything fast. We knew each other for three months, dated for six months, then got engaged, got pregnant, bought a condo, and had a baby within our first year as a couple. I don't regret one minute of how our story unfolded, but I know that we didn't get as much time as other couples do to get to know each other before bringing a baby into the mix, which is the most difficult time in a marriage. It's stressful and emotional and exhausting and messy and joyful and terrifying— and that's on a good day.

When Finn turned thirteen months, I told Colin, "We should start trying for another baby, because what if it takes a while?"

I was already pregnant. I'm fairly sure that happened when we convinced ourselves to get away for a weekend *with the baby*. We found a Groupon for a hotel in Orange County, and I came back with hand, foot, and mouth disease and a pregnancy.

At twenty weeks, I found out I had to go on full bed rest due to a cervical injury during my delivery with Finn. He had torn my cervical O-ring. Colin was an extraordinary human during that time. If you can't tell, I am a high-strung person, so when a doctor told me that I had to have stitches put in my cervix and lie on my back for 110 days so I didn't go into premature labor and lose my baby, it took me a little while to adjust. I was devastated and scared, and I felt ripped off. I wanted to celebrate my pregnancy and show off my perfect belly. I wanted to be pregnant with Jen and go shopping together and have decadent lunches so we could compare pregnancy war stories. But all of that quickly spiraled into the greatest fear I have ever known. I couldn't lose her. I was already in love.

Colin was a hero. He handled me with such care. He put a mini fridge in next to my bed and stocked it full of bagels, cream cheese, chocolate, whatever wouldn't give me heartburn. I wore the same T-shirt for days at a time, and I smelled like a truck stop. He brought me every meal and sat with me while I watched terrible television for hours. He would time my showers and put me back to bed. He followed the rules. He even timed my trips to the bathroom so I wasn't on my feet for too long. He knew I was struggling, and a turning point came when he sat next to me and said, "Kristin, I know this is super hard. But I'm not ready to meet our daughter yet." I started to bawl. Then I lay on my back for the next four months.

Eleanor was born at thirty-eight weeks, happy and healthy. Having a daughter has been the greatest thing to ever happen to Colin. He has only brothers, and at times, I will tell you, Colin can be a bit (a lot) insensitive. But now he has a little girl, and she is his world. Eleanor is sweet to her core, and it dismantles Colin. He can't talk about her without getting choked up. Colin is a big teddy bear, and even Jen's baby daughter knows it. Delilah wanted Colin to hold her all the time when we were on our tour bus last summer, and even though Colin would act bothered, he loved every second of it. We are fairly sure Delilah's first word was "Colin," but we don't talk about it because it's a bit of a sore spot for some other family members.

Colin and I have been together now for almost a decade. I have been with him longer than any other relationship I've ever had. He knows me in every way, and he accepts me as I am. With that being said, he can be annoying AF. Did he clean his ears with a napkin at a restaurant when we were first dating? Yes, he did. Does he still? You better believe it.

Our marriage isn't perfect. Not by a long shot. We are very similar in many ways, which means neither of us will back down from a fight or decide on a restaurant. We fight over super stupid shit that seems very important at the time. Our last argument was because he was giving me notes on how to air-drum properly. Ef him. I air-drum like a pro.

Overall, the big stuff is where we do well. We love being with our kids and doing corny family stuff. He leans into the dad role with ease and enthusiasm. He didn't have a great dad, so it's pretty incredible that he knows how to do this just by following his heart. I can overlook his faults (I will include a detailed list at the end of this book) because he overlooks mine (no list will be included at the end of this book) and because we love each other. Gross. Love makes you gross. And kids are super gross. So it's all gross. It's just nice to be gross in the weeds with someone you love.

JEN

When Brit and I got married, our friend asked us each to make a list of the top ten reasons that we loved each other. When he read the lists at our reception, they were astonishingly similar. We both wrote about the other's ability to make us laugh, the joyous way we start each day, our shared love of savory foods—and we both made jokes about boot knockin'. The one point we made that was worded almost identically was that we will do something difficult with the other just so that our partner doesn't have to do it alone. That's pretty awesome. And even now that we're parents of two toddlers, we do all of our compulsive temperature checking, diaper blowout clean-ups, and irrational screaming together. For all the minor irritations, fundamental disagreements, nightly snoring, and daily farting, my husband and I are both in it for the same reason: everything is better when we do it together.

Don't get me wrong—he's a real idiot, and I say that with love. If you meet Brit, I hope you like puns and dad jokes. His sense of humor is drier than Steven Wright in the Mojave Desert. His delivery can best be described as confusing. I'm constantly having to over-laugh at his jokes when we meet someone new so that they realize he really *is* the father of our children and that he is *not* Michael McDonald of the Doobie Brothers. When I was nine months enormously pregnant, his favorite joke was to tell people I was due in six months. He'll order drinks for me by saying, "My daughter will have the . . . ," and then he'll kiss me on the mouth. It's all delightful.

Meeting him was the luckiest I've ever been, and I don't believe in luck. I believe in ghosts, but luck is for suckers. I have to say, I kissed my fair share of frogs, some lovely gents, some real dirtbags, and even a few dreamboats with some fatal flaws. (That sounds like a lot of kisses. Whatever. It is what it is. I've lived. I didn't meet my husband at nineteen. At least not this one, he's the good one. I've gone down a rabbit hole here. Where was I? Oh, yes, my scandalous, pre-Brit days.) By the time I met Brit, I'd had long stretches of being single and long stretches of codependence. I knew how I like to spend my Friday nights, be they alone or with a companion. I guess what I'm saying is, I know a good one when he comes along.

And one Saturday, about ten years ago, he came along. At first, I was resistant. During my single days, my neighbor Bette had made me write out a very specific list of what I was looking for in a man. I listed everything! What he liked to do, eat, watch, and listen to, that he would love dogs and travel. That he would enjoy chips and salsa as much as I do, and that he would have a huge penis. I wrote that he'd be a kind person who tipped well and believed in horoscopes. I wanted a man who made few grammatical errors, found humor in certain fonts, allowed himself to cry but could also take a punch if need be. I wanted a man who had grown up with a sister so he could respect and fear women appropriately but also know how to play with them in a way that doesn't lead to making out all the time. I hoped he'd find that my mistakes made me evolved and interesting, not flawed. I wished he'd appreciate my old lady taste in film, furniture, and jewelry. Bette told me to set the list under a lavender candle, which she provided, and burn it nightly.

I was living in Venice Beach at the time, because why not? I was single, ready to party, and liked to ride my beach cruiser to the bars. I worked a series of lame advertising jobs over the years, selling print ad space to car dealerships to pay the bills (barely). One sunny afternoon, after having spent seven hours working at the newspaper's booth at the Long Beach Boat and RV Show, I took my dog to the dog park. My dog, Venus, taught me everything I needed to know about love: selflessness, acceptance, and how to sleep with a bed hog. She was the love of my life at the time, so after a long day of being inside while Mommy sold RV ads, she deserved a chance to run through some other dogs' poop and some drug paraphernalia at the Venice Beach Dog Park.

I sat on the top of a picnic bench, which was the only place that had a decent chance of being semi-clean. It was late in the day and turning overcast, so there weren't that many people or dogs at the park. There were plenty of places for someone to sit. But about fifteen minutes into our stay, a dude in ridiculous Air Force 1 Nikes and really stupid sunglasses sat down atop the picnic bench right beside me. I didn't even look in his direction. I'd been batting away middle-aged men in Oakleys and Tommy Bahama shirts at the boat and RV show all day, so no matter how charming this guy looked, I was tapped out. I rolled my eyes and tried to look busy.

He started talking to me about how he'd seen me there before, how most of the people there were mean, crazy, homeless, or a combo of all three. I seemed normal, so why did I come there? I'm sure I replied something witty, because he just started talking and kept at it for an hour. About how he'd just moved there from New York City, how he had won $1,100 at a casino and it was all in his pocket in case he met a girl he wanted to impress, how he had given his dog several names over several weeks before landing on Kaylee, how his mother had passed away when he was twenty-seven and it was the hardest thing in his life, how he was best friends with his sister. He wouldn't shut up. Somehow, we sat there until the sun was setting, laughing and not feeling alone. But then he got up, gave me a hug, and walked home. He didn't get my number, my email, my ham radio handle. He didn't ask if I was on Myspace—he didn't even *get my name.*

I saw him at the dog park about twice a week after that for at least a month. We had friends in common. He had just met a good friend of mine—"Kristin, I think?"—completely separate from me! Venice Beach is in Los Angeles, and Los Angeles has about 14 million people in it. *Are you kidding me? This is such kismet and you still have not even asked for my phone number. I mean, we even hug when we say goodbye, now what the what?*

I was *not* just going to give him my number either. Men are hunters by nature. When they want something, they hunt it down. That's how you know they want it. I was falling for this Dog Park Guy, as all my friends were calling him, but I'll be damned if I was going to just offer up my phone number. Then about five weeks after we met, I got an email with the subject line "Jen?"

It continued: "Jen from the dog park? I got your email from Carrie. I'm having a birthday party next Saturday and you'd be a real idiot if you didn't come.—Brit."

Needless to say, I went. The first several hours of this party were not ideal. I may have drunk chardonnay like it was Gatorade out of nervousness and heat exhaustion. I may have smoked pot in front of Brit's dad. I may have had flaming shots of absinthe. He may have made out with some other girl in his kitchen. He may have been served cake by a different woman I temporarily believed to be his wife. He definitely gave my phone number (which he asked for via email that week) to his friend. It was a disaster. But he did have the good sense to invite me to sushi the next evening, where I quickly listed all the reasons I did not like him and outlined how his birthday party had been a not-so-fun night for me. He laughed. Brit does this super annoying, high-pitched, womanly laugh when he finds something truly funny. He evidently found that night pretty funny, as he scream-laughed through our meal at Hama Sushi. Why had I even agreed to come out with him? Honestly, there was no good reason. Just luck (and maybe my hippie, blues singer neighbor who had made me list what I wanted so I'd know it when it sat down next to me, even if it was wearing Costco sunglasses).

Anyway, that's how he started to date Kristin and me. When Brit and I met, Kristin was fresh from a breakup so, new guy for me or not, I had to keep my eye on her, especially in the evenings. We were generally a threesome (at dinner and drinks

81

only—we aren't *that* fun). My husband has a real back East way about him, which means he feels like he has to pay for everything, or it brings shame on his family or something. So both K and I got courted—package deal, ya know? Everything is better when you do it together! It was very fun for a while. But then Kristin met Colin this one Thursday, and by Tuesday they were engaged and she was pregnant, so our party times came to an abrupt halt. I may have that time line wrong, but I think it's pretty accurate. I didn't even get to weigh in on Colin. Good thing I immediately adored him. Kristin giggled like a schoolgirl at a Bon Jovi concert when she was with Colin, and she never did that, so I figured Colin must have had her number. He must have asked her for it very early on, ahem . . .

Brit and I continued to date. Dating is fun for young people, but it's a job interview when you're getting older. My perspective was *I'm only going to offer you the position once, and then I'm going to look for a candidate who is willing to start immediately.* Brit did not understand this. I kept having to break up with him and remind him that he moved sooooo slowly that I could meet a whole new person and be married to him before he got it together. Sure, I might like this candidate less, he may have, ahem, smaller qualifications, but I was no spring chicken. It took four years and a lot of threats for Brit and me to get engaged.

He took so long to propose, though, that I honestly don't let him weigh in on any important life decisions anymore. Nearly letting a good thing like me slip away? He clearly can't be trusted. Can't risk it. So I told him we would have two kids—a boy and a girl—immediately, and we did. We maybe should have consulted with a third party.

Those kids are my life. I love those turkeys beyond beyond. I don't need to tell you that I'd allow myself to be boiled and peeled for them. However, I just assumed that since so many idiots in the world have kids, it couldn't be that hard. But ef'n geeeeeeeeeeeeeeeeeeez, man. It's hard on every level. Dante's Inferno has nothing on an infant/toddler/parent stomach flu night.

Let's start at the beginning with this baby/kid stuff. Nah, how about a step before that, even, when we were trying to conceive? We lost one baby. I cried every night for a month after our miscarriage. I didn't understand why I was so sad. I kept assuming it was hormones, but I felt so terribly scared that I had done something wrong or was "broken" somehow. I try to share the loss with other women because so many of us have been through it. And if you haven't been through it, it's so hard to explain. I felt like I had been carrying around this wish, and then one day the universe said, "Nope. Just kidding. You can't have this wish." It feels cruel. It is. Don't let anyone tell you it's not. I remember, just days after it happened, having to sit in a meeting at work, wearing this huge pad, exhausted from crying, and having to grit my teeth through a team-building exercise. Are you kidding me? I'll tell you what a team-building exercise is: having a miscarriage and having to rely on your husband to keep you going. Brit nailed it. He let me be crazy, sad, obsessed, disappointed, and angry, and he never judged me. He was physically and emotionally with me for everything, so I didn't have to do it alone.

So, yeah, getting pregnant was a lot harder for us than a broken condom on prom night. But you have never seen a man so committed to getting someone pregnant as my husband. It was as though it was all he thought about. Night and day. He was so selfless. He tried in every manner he could think of, relentlessly trying to put a baby in me. It had to have gotten boring. There must have been times he wanted to give up, but somehow he found the strength deep within himself to get boner after boner, until finally we were pregnant. He's a hero, you guys.

Then when I got pregnant, I don't think he thought it was real until like two weeks before the baby came. Sure, people bought him books, and he scanned them with an interested-looking face because he's polite, but I don't think he read a word. I read everything. Even his dadding books. He was checking sports scores during our birthing class. He was texting his friend Joe during New Baby class. Kristin's husband put our crib together. But some things just come naturally. Brit used to sing to my stomach because it made the baby move in my belly. Because he had not done proper research on baby songs, all he knew how to sing was the ABCs. So almost nightly, as I was so scared of losing this baby after our first pregnancy, I'd make him sing it to my belly button. Because the at-home ultrasound machine I'd purchased wasn't enough. (Oh my goodness, I am bonkers.) When Dashiel was delivered, via C-section, at 3:06 a.m., Brit left my side momentarily to go look at his screaming boy. He didn't know what to do, but he knew that he wanted to make him stop screaming. He started singing the alphabet song to Dash. I could hear it, even though I was deeply under anesthesia and exhausted and trying to explain to my OB that I didn't like Foghat, could he change his iPod, or this would be all I'd remember from my first child's birth? As my husband told me, minutes later in the recovery room, "He stopped crying. He stopped crying and turned to try and see me as soon as I got to 'G.'"

And that is how the World's #1 Dad was born. It's true. I mean, like I said, he's an idiot. I find dirty diapers inside of clean ones inside of onesies inside the dryer sometimes. That's a hat trick. He has to ask me *every time* how much medicine to give them. He has never met their dentist. He doesn't know their shoe size. Their ears would never be cleaned if I didn't do it. I'm seriously leaving that duty to someone in my will. But he's an awesome dad. He's a better parent than I am in many ways. For one, he gets up early with them every morning. Now, we both will get up at night, but it started when I was breast-feeding, and he couldn't help, so he felt kind of guilty. He'd let me sleep in the morning and take that really rough first shift. (I wanted to breastfeed our daughter into her teens for this very reason, but no dice.) For two, maybe my favorite reason, he talks to them like they are adults, respects them, helps them understand, and *then* yells if all of that doesn't work.

Our daughter was born two and a half years after Dash. We had both hoped for a girl, as Brit has a sister and I have a brother, and they are our best friends. We named her Delilah, and she is the happiest person I've ever met. I was worried that if we had a girl, Brit would spoil her rotten. But because the universe likes irony, that baby *owns* me. I am delighted by everything she does, and Brit has to discipline her because I'm incapable of it.

His dedication to our kids can be summed up quite simply: he will snot-suck their noses without the filter part of the device. He doesn't even care if he gets boogs in his mouth if it helps them. Sure, it could be because he didn't read the directions, but still, it takes a real man to suck someone else's boogers directly out of their nose. There have been so many nights where we both got zero hours of sleep, were sick, and had busy schedules the next day, but we worked together to get a fever down, sped to the ER, tried to sleep with barf on our shirts, all the hard stuff. We do it together. I'm very lucky that I decided to force him to marry me.

I LOSE MY MIND SO HARD

Hormones—whose bright idea were those? Let's have some violent, unseeable force manipulate all of a woman's thoughts and behaviors. Let's have them control her sex drive, anger, and acne, and then just see what happens! This is why people thought women were witches. And probably why some women actually became witches. Women have to endure a category 5 hormonal hurricane on the regular, bleed, give birth, and then act like none of it is happening? Bad idea. It's hard enough, man, without an actual chemical bath washing over your brain every time your body goes through something. PMS gets all the glory here, but you know what *really* lets hormones show their true power? Giving birth. Making a tiny human does a number on your brain. You want to do a complete one-eighty on your neurochemistry? Have yourself a baby. You'll cycle through sadness, anger, and joy faster than super-plus tampons on day three. A woman endures excruciating physical pain, isolation, and starvation when giving birth. You know what you call a man who goes through all of that? *A Navy SEAL.*

Everyone keeps telling you that this is the most joyous part of your life, but meanwhile you're recovering from either a horizontal or vertical tear down there and crying so hard you break a rib. You can call it the baby blues if you want, but that's way too cute of a name for what most women feel—though you would never know it from the way most people talk about it. Or don't talk about it. There is a weird code of silence about how deeply shitty the period right after childbirth can be. In contrast, men mention their broken boners a few times, and it's *bring on the commercials featuring silver foxes lounging lustily in outdoor bathtubs.* Men get *almost* a cold and they think they're dying, but moms experience an actual chemical/hormonal apocalypse and they protest, "No, I'm fine. I'm fine." But, you guys, there's no shame in it. And you are most definitely not fine and most definitely not alone.

No one wants to come out and say it because it will seem ungrateful, but coming home from the hospital is not the happiest time of your life. It's terrifying, isolating, confusing, painful, emotional, and physically impossible. Okay, yes, there is joy sprinkled in there too, but you're leaking from places that used to be your good-time spots. You can't eat anything that requires a utensil. And the creature you brought home makes you *feel* so much that you almost can't contain it. You will find yourself ugly-scream-crying, "I love you so effing much!" Oh, and people are gonna ask when your baby is due for five months after you've given birth.

Yay.

JEN

I think every mom gets PPD. Even if you don't have your brain chemistry all out of whack and it's not PPD, you probably at least get hit with PPWTF just happened?

It's so normal. I don't ask anyone if they are a little depressed after birth anymore. I just assume that they are. In fact, if a new mom looks like she's doing a really great job, I know I need to intervene. She's gone off the deep end. Not every mom ends up clinically depressed, but there's nothing like standing in the shower while every liquid that's in your body flows out of it to humanize you a little bit. It's humbling, to say the least. Everyone needs a little "attagirl" to get them through this period.

I remember sitting in my nursing glider, holding my son while it felt like he was stabbing me in the nipple. What was he doing? I don't know, but it hurt. I'd just been sawed in half and an attached organism was pulled out of my choo choo. Rocking there, I thought, *How has anyone survived this time? How do we still exist as a species?* It's *hard* on every level.

If you're not overwhelmed, if you don't want to run from the house screaming sometimes, if you don't want to put your husband in a sleeper hold, then you are a better woman than I. Or a better liar than I. I felt so below average because it seemed to me that all the other moms had it figured out. Now I know that it's just that moms don't like to post Instagram photos of themselves with backne while they're crying in the car and dipping fries in a Frosty from Wendy's.

So many moms are confused about why they feel this way. It doesn't make sense. It feels like it comes out of nowhere. Might I suggest something crazy? Could it be that you're going through a bit of PTSD from, oh, I dunno, physical and emotional warfare? Many births are flat-out traumatic. You're deprived of food and sleep, you get your insides ripped out, and you find yourself in a room with a small version of yourself stuck to your (suddenly porn star–size) boob, and then you're back in your car before you know what happened. It's like you're Sigourney Weaver, but you're forced to take the alien home with you. That's not normal, but all you're allowed to say about it is "Whew, that was a long day. Forgive me for being a little shaken up." Plus, instead of nurturing yourself for a while, you have to tackle a physical task that is the equivalent of doing a Tough Mudder with a butt tear from 1:00 a.m. to 4:00 a.m. every night for a couple of years, while you're doubling as a snack bar around the clock. And you're not supposed to cry sometimes? Fuuucck you.

It's disorienting. Even once you're home, back on familiar ground, it still feels like a strange land. You are just exhausted, physically and emotionally. My postpartum weeks made the depression I had suffered before look like winning an all-expenses-paid vacation to Hawaii.

Expectation versus reality can really mess with your head during this time. You want those early days with your newborn to be picture perfect, but it's more like a picture that some-one barfed on, won't let go of, and is trying to shove into their mouth again. Thanks, magazines and baby photographers, for making me think I should be back to my pre-baby size a week after coming home, wearing a white dress while I hold my sweet baby with a crown of daisies on her head. If you had taken a photo of me a week after giving birth, I would have been lying facedown on a carpet covered in diarrhea. And that would have been on a good day. Don't ask me how I'm doing—just bring me coffee and doughnuts and don't count how many I eat.

Women think that if they have PPD they're going to hurt the baby. For me, I didn't think I'd hurt the baby, but I certainly wanted to hurt my husband. After I had my son, I was so scared to do anything but smile at him all day to show him that he was loved unconditionally that after I put him to bed I'd just stare at a wall, expressionless. My husband would ask, "Are you okay?" And I'd snap, "Shut up. What are you, the police? Leave me alone. What are you suggesting? Stop judging me." Then one day I chucked a full yogurt container at his face, and I thought, *Oh hey, I don't usually do that . . . I should probably go to the doctor.*

On the outside, though, it's showtime. You're Donna Reed meets Martha Stewart meets Gwyneth Paltrow in full Goop mode. When friends stop by, you're like, "Come on in, I was just mixing up a batch of cookies. Would you like some?" Meanwhile, your nursing bra is on top of your shirt and your phone is in the freezer.

Your paranoia that you're doing things wrong is off the damn charts. Instead of sleeping when I could, I would worry about how everything I had ever done would come back to haunt me or the baby. If it's something you can get paranoid about, I've researched it. Do you know that kids can get hair wrapped around their toe or penis and lose circulation in it? Now you do. You're welcome. While I worried, I stayed up late at night breastfeeding and reading *The Devil in the White City*, trying to decide whether I should build a fortress to keep my child indoors for the rest of his life or just go all in and move to a remote island to protect him from civilization.

You second-guess everything, trying to follow all the advice so you don't screw things up. You're determined not to mess up this kid by being . . . well, a normal person with thoughts and feelings and needs. I busted my butt trying to maintain eye contact while I changed diapers because I wanted him to develop healthy attachment. I was sure I hit brain every time I cleaned an ear. I was positive my breastmilk had pot in it from ten years ago. One morning, I took off my son's diaper and there was another diaper underneath it.

And it wasn't just baby paranoia: I thought my husband might leave me for some hot woman, and then I thought, *Eh, that's never been his type.*

The problem with reading as many parenting books as I did was that I thought my kid had all these delays. Would he ever roll over, sit up, coo? What would I do if he didn't? Were there rollover specialists? The good news is that there's nothing like a second kid to cure all that. The only milestone we celebrated the second time around was when she learned how to use the remote.

No matter how much reading you do, you're unprepared. Before Dash was born, I read this article that said we need fourteen outfits for the first month of the baby's life. By 4:30 in the morning of our first night at home, I looked at my husband and said, "There are no more clothes left." And we just laughed hysterically, found the least-disgusting onesie, and wrestled him back into that.

Husbands get their own version of PPD: post-parenting denial. They've been waiting in monk mode for months, and they're all nervous about bringing up the prospect of having sex again. They work up the courage to get a little friendly, and when they do, it's like they're speaking a foreign language. "Sex? You've got to be kidding me. This is a whole new vagina and neither of us has read the owner's manual. Who knows what will happen, but if history is any indication, it will be something very humbling for me."

Being a new parent hit my husband hard in other ways too. He lost his mind a little bit as well. He wasn't as cuckoo town as I was, but he would wake up in the middle of the night looking under the bed for the baby. I knew the baby wasn't there, but I was also so freaked out I got down on the floor and looked with him anyway. You just don't trust yourself. And maybe you shouldn't, 'cause you act bananas. My husband even felt guilty that he wasn't paying as much attention to the dogs as he used to. One afternoon, I walked into our dark bedroom holding the baby and I heard this breathy, creepy "Jennnnnnn" from behind the door. I screamed and peed. And then screamed and peed again. My husband was super apologetic—he had simply been trying to play hide-and-go-seek with our Australian shepherd and was trying to warn me that he was behind the door without tipping her off. Okay, cool. Totally normal.

The weirdest thing is how damn hard it is to say, "Hey, I need help." I tried. I got as far as "Hey," a couple of times, but then *ffzzzzzt*. People try to help. They love to tell you that you should exercise. My response to that is "No, *you* should exercise. Like run right now. Because I'm going to use my last bit of energy to choke the life out of you."

It didn't occur to me that it was PPD. I thought PPD meant I was going to Thelma and Louise my way right off a cliff with my baby in the back seat. But I didn't want to kill myself—I was just mad. Really, really mad. All the time. I finally admitted that I needed help. I summoned the nerve to go to the doctor so I could confess that I had lost my flipping mind, and she said, "Seriously? You don't know what this is? Maybe you should read some books." (Apparently, I should have read some books about what was happening with *me*, not just the baby.) She tore off a couple of scripts, and said, "In seven years, you're going to have a nice laugh about this, but for now a little medication will fix you right up," and you know what, you guys? It did. After about a week, I was thinking, *Wait, is this what normal people feel like?* and I started to feel okay. So I say, if meds are going to help you, why not? Go get some.

Kristin also went a little off her rocker after she had Eleanor. Instead of going to the doctor, she handled it by doing what we all do when we're completely overwhelmed: she signed up for scuba lessons.

KRISTIN

Yeah, it may not have been the most rational decision I've ever made. But when Eleanor was five weeks old, I signed up for scuba lessons for me and my husband. I told Jen about it, and she squinted at me for a while trying to figure out *Is she* *being a wiseass or an idiot?* before she came out with "What in the actual f*ck are you talking about? I love you, but that is straight-up bonkers." It was the first time she had ever talked to me like that. I don't know what I was thinking. I couldn't even figure out how to set the coffee maker in the morning, but I felt like I wanted to reconnect with my husband, and learning to breathe underwater felt like just the ticket. Jen said, "How about you guys, oh, I don't know, raise a baby together and connect over that?" I was like, "I know, I know. Okay, gotta go, I have to take this test to calculate the percentage of nitrox the body can tolerate at different depths!"

Jen thought I was crazy. Jen *knew* I was crazy. I was crazy. I had been on bed rest for 110 days with Eleanor. It was the most difficult and emotional time of my life, and when I was given the green light to go back to regular movement, I literally went off the deep end.

I got through one class, and I came to my senses. "Okay, fine. Everyone here is twenty-two, and no one has children. What am I doing?" To qualify for the class I had to swim ten laps and tread water for what felt like fifteen hours. I nearly drowned. My body was traumatized from a C-section and I had lost so much muscle by lying down for 110 days—and swimming is really effing hard. It was just really cloudy thinking. I mean, where would we be going scuba diving anyway, Babies "R" Us? We wouldn't even be getting on a plane in the next few years. I was cuckoo for Cocoa Puffs.

I should have known I'd go a little nuts right after Eleanor's birth. I'd suffered from PPD and OCD after I had Finn. As we mentioned before, I had horrible thoughts that I was going to hurt my baby. For instance, I had the unshakable repetitive thought that if I walked from one room to the next I would hit his sweet little baby head on the door jamb and his head would explode. That is not how we are designed, you guys. There is no self-destruct button on an infant's skull. But I loved that helpless little dude so much that all I could think about was the bajillion ways he could die. I did the finger-under-the-nose test a thousand times on my son, so much that he finally looked at me like, *Back off, lady.*

Eventually, I did hit his head on the door (What can I say? Doors are hard to navigate when you're bone-tired), and his skull did not spontaneously combust. It pissed him off, but he didn't die. He was fine. Of course he was fine. It was just a little bump on the noggin, not a life-changing catastrophe, and thank God because I do it to myself like twelve times a day.

I think we all feel the need to say the same thing when we are asked how we are doing after we have a baby. We all chirp back, "Oh, it's good." But you can see the pain and a little bit of crazy in the eyes of your girlfriends who have just become new moms. What New Mom really wants to say to you, but is too afraid, is "Bitch, you should've told me it would be insanely hard." Your brain is f*cking with you on every level. I burned 1,200 calories a day from the sheer force of my crying after each of my kids was born. I had good eaters, good sleepers, but I just wasn't happy. I didn't wear pants for eight weeks. And it's not like babies are bringing a lot to the party when they first show up. They just lie there and poop. But you have so much to do. It's impossible to comprehend before you have a baby, but being responsible for keeping another creature alive is so much damn work.

There is so much recalculating you have to do. Not only is your sleep schedule a joke, your body leaking, and your ability to speak coherently gone, but modesty goes out the window. Before I had kids, if you had told me that I was going to walk around with no shirt on while my mother-in-law was in the room, I would have laughed so hard at you that you would have thought I was mean. Now, she could tell you the exact size and shape of my areolas.

You know what helped, though? Jen. She came over when Finn was born and insisted I get out of the house. She said, "I don't know anything about babies, but I know the number for 911," and I said, "Good enough for me." Jen and the baby watched *Gangland* together, and I went out with my husband and felt ever so slightly sane again just being out in the world, navigating it like an adult with a brain that was semi-functional. I'll never forget that she did that for me.

Sometimes I'm asked, "What was the one thing that someone bought for you that, as a new mom, you couldn't do without?" You wanna know what I say? I say that I didn't need a Diaper Genie or a bottle warmer. I just needed some laughs and a friend. Someone to load the dishwasher, order a pizza. Or gently put my hair behind my ear (that's what Jen does, and I instantly cry). Someone to rub my shoulders, hug me, and tell me I wasn't losing my mind—because I felt *totally lost*.

It makes me furious when people talk about postpartum depression like it's a weakness or a fleeting whimsical moment. We should literally tell every woman, "This will happen." The darkness is real. And it's normal. And there is zero shame. For some women it's a little less, and for some it's a lot more. No woman should be made to feel ashamed for being overwhelmed. We brewed a human. And then we pushed it or had it taken out of us. It's brutal and catastrophic. New Mom, next time someone asks you, "How's it all going?" just reply honestly in that moment: "I haven't slept for eight days, I nearly blew my asshole after my first poop since the baby, and I spontaneously cry all day." And if that woman is a mother, she'll look at you and say, "Yes. That seems about right." (Side note: If you see a mom who is *really* struggling, then take her to the doctor. Ain't no shame in a pharmaceutical game if it means that mama is taken care of. We can only be good to others if we are good to ourselves first.)

This is where I would like to open this conversation to all mothers, aunties, friends, all kinds of mothers. If you adopted or find yourself with bonus kids, you are not excluded from this conversation. The minute you choose to love another being, you will find yourself feeling scared and confused just like everyone else. We mothers are nurturing, loving, selfless—sometimes at our own peril.

The point is that we have to take care of one another and never assume that anyone has it all figured out. We can all use extra love and support and laughter, especially laughter, during those hard days. Reach out, make a friend, lend a hand, especially to a new mom. Go over. Watch the baby. Or the other kids. Bring over a coffee and a stain stick. "Here's a casserole, some chocolate, and some judgment-free clothes folding." Tell her, "You're not crazy. It gets better. Now, go shower. Go nap. *Just go.*" Even you single ladies, like my friend Laura, who at the time didn't have babies. But she came over and gave me her time and loved on me and the kids. She is Eleanor's godmother, and she was a godsend. And ladies, if *you* are the new mom, then just say thank you and pay it forward.

I MOM FRIEND SO HARD

Have you ever gone on vacation to a place where they don't speak English and everything is just a little bit harder than you'd like it to be? Like figuring out where the bathroom is or ordering fish that's been cooked? It's exhilarating and stimulating . . . and totally exhausting. But then you see another tourist and he's wearing a shirt with your hometown's football team on it, and when you chat him up on the autobus it's like you found a tiny island where you can relax. He gets you. That's what it's like when you find a good mom friend. She totally speaks your language. You can take your proverbial bra off around her (and your real one too).

As important as it is to have a partner who co-parents in sync with you, your mom friend is your real lifeline. She's your teacher, your confidante, your partner in crime, and your parole officer all rolled into one. She's there when you just need someone to tell you that you're not nutso for crying when you find a tiny sock that your kid can't fit in anymore. Or that it's okay to give your kid an iPad for six hours straight to survive a cross-country flight—or dinner in a nice restaurant. Or that you are not the worst mom ever for feeling like it's all just too much sometimes.

It's like that exotic vacation. It's supposed to be amazing all the time, but navigating the unfamiliar territory can make you long for the comforts of home. Part of being a mom is summoning up the courage to open the door a crack to let other people know that motherhood is not at all what you thought it was going to be. It's brutal and beautiful all at once—and no one appreciates that like another mom.

KRISTIN

I'm not good at a lot of things, but one thing I like to brag about is the collection of lady friends I have acquired through the years. Friendship is the only way to survive motherhood. You have to have someone who understands that every time you sneeze you pee or that you screamed at your kid for wearing the same shirt twice or that sometimes it feels good to google "divorce." Your mom friends are not blood, they are chosen, and they are more important than any other relationship in your life. There, I said it.

I am still very close with friends I went to preschool with, obviously Jen and I are married, and I am rapidly becoming closer with the new mom friends I made just this year. I take pride in my internal detection device that will immediately tell me, "This is a good one. Come on strong." I am acutely aware that we are the company we keep, so if a person doesn't make me feel good or sets off an alarm in my gut zone, I immediately retreat. However, if you have mascara on from yesterday or visible panty lines, we will be best friends. If I can see you crying in your car or quiet-yelling at your kid with a clenched jaw and a cold latte, I'm all yours. I need real. I need honest. I need funny. I would love to tell you how inspired, or motivated, or uplifted, or intellectually stimulated I am by all of my friends, but at the end of the day I love them because they make me laugh.

I *live* to belly laugh. You know the laugh, the one where you can't breathe, your face turns red and blotchy, you cry— and pee—a lot. You probably have your hands up fanning your face to dry the tears. It's better than an orgasm, because a belly laugh can stay with you for days. You'll be in the middle of folding clothes and you'll think about what tickled you and start to laugh all over again. Unfortunately, that is not how orgasms work.

Moms get told that what we do is trivial or boring or unsexy. Moms are constantly put into the least cool box. Nobody cares about how you were able to get slime out of your daughter's hair except another mom. Moms understand the day-to-day struggles, but they also understand the mental warfare. No mother is perfect, and it's nice to have someone to pick you up when you fall. Or when your kid falls.

When my son was four months old, I wedged him between two pillows on my bed and I went into the other room to grab the laundry so I could fold it on the bed. In less than thirty seconds,

Finn somehow dislodged himself and fell off the bed. He screamed. I screamed. He bawled. I bawled. I called the doctor. She said, "This happens so often we ask that you *do not* come in to the office." Finn calmed down and was fine. Not even a bruise. But I started destroying myself mentally. How could I let this happen? So I called my friend Lynn in Nebraska who has four grown boys. She said, "Oh, all of my kids fell down the stairs as babies, and one of them fell out of the car. They bend; they don't break." She made me feel like I could forgive myself, and we laughed. I felt a tiny bit less alone in that moment.

The truth is that motherhood can be lonely. That seems impossible, right? The definition of motherhood is that there is someone else always depending on you so you are literally *never* alone. There is this little creature who relies on you, and you *should be happy*. But that is not the reality. The reality is that our minds, our hearts, our perceptions, our personalities, and our fears all shift when we become mothers. (BTW, this includes all mothers, not just the ones who delivered the kid.) Nothing, I repeat, nothing is ever the same. At the core of all of it is love, and the love is almost as hard to endure as the pain. No one ever has a baby, looks at it, and goes, "Meh. I'm a little disappointed. I thought he'd have more hair." You look at that baby, and no matter how red or misshapen or gooey he is, you think, *I am so in love it hurts*.

You never feel truly qualified. No one ever says, "Oh, sure, I have this motherhood thing nailed." Yet we try. And we fail. And the failure is relentless and daily and painful. Sometimes it's a first step into a very, very dark place. We have all been there. We have all wondered how we will survive. Sometimes we wonder if we should. Here's the good news: you are never alone. There isn't one thought you have had that someone else hasn't. It's true. No matter how dark, disgusting, perverse, or terrifying the thought, some other woman has had that one too. That's why we need mom friends. Because they understand the darkness. And if your friend is a good one, she will look at you and say, "I get it."

And that leads me to Jen. After we both moved to Los Angeles and were in the thick of studying and performing comedy, I went to a comedy show at a terrible theater that was so poor it called itself The Salon, simply because the space used to be a salon and keeping the name was cheaper than changing the sign. It also smelled like perm. Jen performed that night, and I was one of eight audience members. I remember that Jen was really funny and wore a lot of accessories. I thought, *How does she do anything with so many necklaces, earrings, and bracelets?* But she did, and she did it with ease.

My friend Jenny (I have many Jens, Jennis, and Jennys in my life) remembers when Jen and I met. She was standing next to us when we figured out we were both from Nebraska. Jenny (not Jen) said we were both using voices that would shatter glass. "How do we not know each other?" we squealed. Once we started to unlock the puzzle, we found out that not only did we know all the same people, but Jen and I lived a block apart and both drove MINI Coopers like real assholes. It was a little ridiculous, but we fell in love that night, and I knew immediately that I would be her friend for life.

Jen and I were very good friends, but both of us had pretty active lives without each other. We were both performing comedy all over town. She was really involved with the Groundlings, and I was in a sketch improv team through Second City. We had lots of friends outside of one another but always managed to circle back and find ourselves laughing at all the pitfalls of trying to make it in comedy. Jen always makes the joke that having kids should have been a real cooler for our comedy careers, but it actually helped. From the get-go, it was obvious that our friendship was the kind that gets better with age.

I adore Jen on a thousand different levels. She is pretty, feminine, and warm, has great style and very cute small-person hands. She eats terrible food, she salts the shit out of everything, and her coffee tastes like a milkshake. She loves to sparkle but will only get something if it's on sale or it's free in a dumpster. She's delicate but not a shrinking violet. She is tender but drives like a bat outta hell. She's so small, but that doesn't mean she's weak. Jen was raised in a military town, and I'd put money on her in a bar fight.

Jen is one million wonderful things, but my favorite thing about her is that she makes me laugh. She is deeply funny and disturbed. And when I'm with her I smile a very unattractive gummy smile and laugh like an old barfly who has a cigarette hanging out of her mouth. It's the kind of laugh I talked about earlier where I can't breathe and I sweat a lot. We are so different in so many ways, but we have so much fun together that it's ridiculous that joking and getting real about motherhood is now how we pay the bills.

The amazing thing about our friendship is what has happened to us after we created a business. Within weeks of our first video, Jen and I were working no less than eighty hours a week on top of momming. I'm the early bird, and she's the night owl, so collectively one of us was working well past midnight (Jen) and one of us was up before 6:00 (me). We carve out time for mommy duties in the morning, work like dogs all day, make dinner, do baths and bedtime, and get back to it at night. Lots of women do this—we aren't so special—but the shift from what we were doing to what we do now was a big one. At one point I remember thinking, *Wow, our company is growing so fast, and that is awesome, but what happens if we spend too much time together? Will our friendship suffer? Is it worth it?* Nothing will test a friendship like business partnership. But in so many ways we were built for this.

It's very easy to get wrapped up in deadlines, posting, schedules, editing, writing, managing business, networking—and we never want to seem ungrateful or like we take a second of this journey for granted. So sometimes, I forget to keep my eye on the ball in terms of what's really important, and Jen helps me with that. For example, we were particularly busy around the time of Eleanor's preschool graduation. Jen and I were both overworked and frenzied, trying hard to hit our deadlines. I called her to tell her my plan: "Jen, if I work in the morning, then I can make it to the graduation. I'll jump on a conference call in the car on the way back, and then I'll skip the graduation party." Jen responded in a low and steady voice, "No. No, you will *not* do that." Her voice lowered again: "You will go to Eleanor's graduation, and you go to her party. Everything else can wait." I started to cry, and I was able to dive back into some very special mommy time, which I desperately needed.

Contrary to popular opinion, women are extraordinary partners in business. Women are more likely to defend their friend than they are to defend themselves. At the core, we are all mama bears, regardless of whether you have cubs or not. It's an "I've got your back and you've got mine" mentality. When Jen and I are faced with a decision, the clearest and best choice comes to me after I ask the question "Do I want this for *us*?" I would take on a lot more if I asked, "Do I want this for myself?" That's why partnership, in particular among women, is so powerful. Women are incredible team players. We navigate with integrity, and if anyone gets hungry we have loads of snacks and juice boxes in our purse to boot.

Because we have been together for as many hours as we have, we can read each other's tells. When I am nervous, Jen says I tap my hands and shift in my seat. When Jen is unsure, she looks up as if she's searching for information and slowly says, "Oh, okay . . ." That's usually a tell that she doesn't like what's happening. I know it immediately because we just get each other.

At the end of the day, we share a mutual love and respect for each other, and we always prioritize family first. I kiss on her kids like they are my own. I delight in seeing them grow. I held Dashiel when he was a newborn and now he looks exactly like his dad. And Delilah cracks me up because she runs like a Muppet, like her mom. This might make you want to throw up, but my kids love her kids, and her kids love my kids, so it's all pretty great. Jen is so wonderful to my kids, and they just adore her. In fact, Eleanor asked if Jen's family could move in with us just so she could see Dashiel and Delilah every day. Eleanor was *not* happy when Jen had to explain that it wouldn't work out.

One of the greatest things about Jen's whole brood is that

whenever we get together, it's easy. Nobody feels like they have to clean the house first or cook fancy food (pizza is a must), the kids can play until they pass out, and we can shoot the shit about anything. It's still like that, and we spend more time together than most conjoined twins. I know. I'm making myself want to throw up too.

JEN

I'm sure it goes without saying that I've made mistakes. We all do, but I've made some pretty epic ones and sometimes on a regular basis. There's one, I hate to admit, that I was guilty of for years, pretty consistently. I kind of wrote off my friends once they became moms.

I was the late bloomer among my group of friends. Everyone had found love and a positive pregnancy test *much* earlier (like ten years earlier) than I did.

In my early thirties, one of my close friends got pregnant and I said out loud, like an asshole, to my then boyfriend, "Well, we have to find a new couple to hang out with. Now that they have a baby, we'll never see them again." And I really thought that. In my defense, I wasn't trying to be a jerk. What I thought was *They have this wonderful, magical baby, so why on earth would they want to hear about my career fails and lack of money?* It never crossed my mind that my friends who had recently become moms might actually desperately *need* me.

Anytime a friend had a baby, I'd send texts, leave messages, and buy expensive baby shoes (I didn't know they'd never get used or even stay on a baby's feet), and then I'd stay out of the new mom's hair. I was also really terrible at holding babies. I was so scared that I'd drop them that when friends would ask if I wanted to hold their young one, I'd say, "No, no. Thanks. No. You break it, you buy it. I'll just look." When I got really brave, I would sit in a low chair and have them place the baby in my arms for about fifteen seconds. That was it.

What was I thinking?!

Those early days of motherhood are hard. Not everybody has family nearby to help, and—news flash!—family isn't always helpful. My father-in-law came after the birth of my first, ate all the food in my freezer, went to the museum, and got massages. My mom, on the other hand, made sure I ate and slept, and then she took lots of photos. She also cleaned and ran the washing machine constantly. My sister-in-law came for a visit and held the baby for exactly one week straight. Perfection. If you have a mom friend, get over there and just start cleaning and holding babies.

Here's what I do now: show up. Unannounced. With a huge bottle of water to set next to her feeding chair or nightstand. I bring a pizza delivery gift card. I bring a big-ass box of the hugest, most absorbent pads that will fit in her pants. I bring champagne. I bring cookies. I bring *Us Weekly* and *People* magazines. I give them the bag, hold that baby, and tell my mom friend to get in the shower. She needs me. And she needs a shower.

That's the big question that nobody knows to ask in baby-care classes before the baby comes: What do I do with a one-week-old when I need to shower? Answer: you buy one of those vibrating bouncing chairs that cost $20, strap the baby in, and shower with the curtain open. Repeat this every other day for one year.

When Kristin had Finn, I didn't have my own kids yet. I knew when she was on her way to the hospital. I said prayers and then anxiously waited for the newborn baby photos. I waited. And waited. Texted her husband to make sure all was okay. And waited. Then, finally, I saw that Finn was born healthy and huge—from Kristin's mom's Facebook page. Okay, I got it. I was always a good friend, but not inner circle. That's fine.

Kristin had a C-section and looked like she had had the crap beaten out of her when I stopped by. I dropped off a stuffed monkey to go with his jungle nursery (to put in a crib? What am I, a psycho?) and a couple of onesies and said, "Let me know if you need anything." And then I just laid low, you know, "out of the way." I really didn't think I could be of any use. I might as well go have sushi, stay out too late, and sleep in in the morning, because I didn't have kids. It looked like I had lost another friend to an adorable, I mean ridiculously adorable, baby. I couldn't compete. (Yes, against a baby. I told you I'm an asshole.)

Kristin sent pictures, some really misspelled texts, including a couple that were meant for other people, but whatever. It was nice to be sort of involved in this world that I didn't fully understand. But I definitely was missing my friend. So one day, when Finn was about six weeks old, I called and said, "Do you want to come over? Or we could come over there? Whatever is easy. I'd just love to see you. Finn can sleep in our room and we can chat." I barely got the words out when I heard tires screech out front.

My front door flung open, and Kristin and Colin, looking very tired but happy, burst in with Finn in a car seat. They set him on our table, grabbed a beer out of the fridge, and said, "We are *so happy* to be out of the house!" She needed *me*!

Yeah . . . I should've just gone over there.

A few months later, I made the sheepish offer, "I could come watch Finn tonight if you guys wanted to get out alone and grab dinner. I don't know much about babies, but I will call 911 if I think it's even remotely necessary." She took me up on it. "Be here in ten minutes." She gave me a quick briefing on feeding and burping, and then they left for Benihana. Finn and I did fine. He barfed on me, he didn't sleep, and we watched *Gangland* for three hours. But the great part was that those guys needed the break, and I needed to be needed.

Kristin had her second and I had my first five weeks apart. It was so exciting! Kristin had to go on bed rest and I overate to the point that movement was difficult, so we were only able to text. When your baby is born, it is all such a blur. I think you have this psychogenic fugue that you go into: for about four months, you don't know who you are, what's going on in the world, or how to have a conversation. You can't remember jack either. I remember two things from that time. Kristin's baby sprinkle for Eleanor was the first time I left the house alone after my son was born (and I only made it like an hour away from the baby). Then, about a week later, my husband, new baby, and I drove to Kristin's and met Eleanor. She was so perfect. Just a bunch of circles put together with a smile in the middle. She was nibbling at her hands like a bunny. She was the cutest baby I'd ever seen. Still true, and I have two of my own now.

All this time, it was never me against a baby. It was every mom against the universe. *Moms need one another.* Everyone else will think you're crazy or complainy or ungrateful, but a mom friend will say, "Look at how perfect that baby is. How can something so cute be so sinister?"

I learned a lot about being a mom from Kristin. She started before I did, and I saw that she was doing a great job of it. It was a shock to know that she didn't feel that way. It was a relief to know that I had a friend who didn't make me feel like I had to pretend I was doing it even close to correctly. In those early months, I had in Kristin, and still have, a person who will tell me it will all be okay. Even when I feel like I'm drowning in a heap of failure and exhaustion, she reminds me that I'm doing okay. And "okay" is a passing score. Kristin is willing to laugh at herself and me. Having her in my life has felt like having a big sister. Like a much, much, much older sister. Around her, I could relax, not be overly precious with everything, ask for help. That's not vulnerable—at least not in a negative way. That's brave.

We're women; we can do it all—or we feel like we can anyway. If we're on fire, we'd rather figure it out on our own than bear the shame of someone seeing us with singed bangs. Let's flip that script. Ask for help. Accept help. Offer help. Force your help on someone. They need it.

Go out and get a mom friend, whether you're a mom or not. Be vulnerable. Be honest. Be understanding. And bring beer.

I KEEP IT TOGETHER SO HARD

How tired are you right now? Does going to the dentist sound amazing because you might get to close your eyes for an entire minute? Did you try to write a check using a stray tampon you found in your purse, thinking it was a pen? When was the last time you read something that wasn't an allergy warning?

Before you become a parent, you kind of know that having kids is supposed to change everything, but you think that when people say that, they mean your heart is going to grow three sizes like the Grinch's and that you'll trade in your MINI Cooper for a minivan. That seems doable. What is impossible to comprehend is how much *work* it is to have a kid. You are Just. So. Busy. All. The. Dang. Time. Before kids, there are whole days in your planner that just say "Brunch." Hilarious. After kids, you learn that spoilers only spoil things for moms, because they're the ones who are never going to be caught up on anything, even TV.

If there is one word that captures motherhood, it's not "exalting." It's "exhaustion." Being this tired all the time is torture. Men have confessed to crimes that they did not commit because they were kept awake for twenty-four hours. If you put a mom in an interrogation room, she'll last four and a half years. *Are you kidding? You want to put me in solitary confinement? A space to myself that's dark where I can nap? Oh, please, anything but that. You want to interrogate me? I have all day. What are you going to do, put some hot lights on? Bring endless cups of coffee? Ask adult questions? Is this an interrogation room or the Radisson?*

KRISTIN

Between working full-time and trying to be a parent all the time, there's just no time. It's no wonder I have a goatee. When am I supposed to take care of that? From the minute I wake up, I think to myself, *Just make it to 7:30.* For most of the day, I'm wiped, and then at about 4:00 or 5:00, I give myself a pep talk—*You're almost there!*—and I start feeling zippy and a little hopeful. *Just a few more hours until I can sink into my sofa with my fat pants and a glass of wine, and watch some Hulu.*

Until then, it's "Finn, clean up your Legos." "Eleanor, go pee-pee potty. I know you say you don't have to go, but you do." "Finn, clean up your Legos." "Eleanor, just breathe." "Colin, queue up *Homeland.*" "Finn, clean up your *Legos.*" "Eleanor [*staring at each other and breathing so she can pee*]. Good girl. Wipe your gina." *"FINN, CLEAN UP YOUR—"* Then stories in bed for Eleanor, skip six pages. Run over to help Finn "read" a book (he reads one page, I read seven). "Mommy, I want water." Okay. "I want *cold* water." Okay. "Mommy, I want—" *OKAY.* "Let's say prayers." *Sweet Jesus, let this night be over.* "God bless Mommy and Daddy and Finn and Eleanor and Dead Grandpa Greg." *Ugh, that feels harsh. Let's move on.* "Why did he die?" "Because he ate bad food. Let's talk about it tomorrow." This is the storm before the calm.

Then, finally, I sit down and it's quiet. My body goes, *Oh yeah, girl.* And then I hear, "Mommy?" *Noooooooooo.* It's not fair. It's like working as a nurse's aide for a nice old man and clocking out and then he asks for just one more thing and you have to work fifteen more minutes for free because it's the right thing to do. But it still sucks.

Before kids, life was carefree. After kids, it's care-full—like I have to care for others fully. I wanted the job, I signed up for the position, but nobody ever really tells you that you will work countless hours of unpaid overtime. Do you remember, when you were young and single, you would wake up on a weekend, ya know, whenever, and you'd sit up in bed and stretch and think, *What do I want to do today? Maybe a movie, maybe I'll work out, maybe drinkies with Jen. Who knows?* You had all the time in the world, but now your time is no longer your own. That is why we sit in our cars for ten minutes before leaving the school parking lot on Monday mornings because, for the first time in days, we get a few minutes to ourselves. It feels so glorious to just not think for a bit. To let yourself wander online, to think about useless, worthless, mindless garbage. We are tired, and we are overworked, and we are often ignored—and the demands never end.

I'm not necessarily hitting it out of the park in the spouse department either. My husband's generally some shade of pissy with me because he feels neglected, which, translated, means he wants to have sex more often. Dude, I have to help Finn prep for a presentation on hot air balloons. What am I supposed to say? "Just hop on while I finish coloring this balloon? Oh, you're game? Great. Okay, but here's the deal. Instead of talking dirty, can you just keep reminding me that I need to sign Eleanor's permission slip?"

When they're babies, you think that's as bad as it's going to get because you cannot imagine anything needier and more demanding than a newborn. You stare at them thinking, *Why is this hard? Like, why?* They just lie there in the bassinet. It's not like they come out and start tap dancing and ask you to solve a riddle. They are just cute little blobs that stare at your boobs and have zero arm control. How did this tiny thing disrupt my life so much? This is supposed to be pretty basic, right? They cry when they are hungry, tired, or wet. It seems simple enough, and yet, that's the Matrix of it all; it's simple but never easy. Then you start doing the math and you realize, *Oh right, it's because I'm nursing twenty-something hours a day, and I'm trying to keep this kid's butt clean, and I'm beyond exhausted. I'm mentally insane, I'm hungry, I'm lonely, and I don't remember one thing about my life prior to this. I'm going to go to bed and get three hours of sleep and do this all again tomorrow.* There is nothing harder.

And I've had it relatively good. Finn was a big baby, he was a strong eater, and I had tons of milk. I did it by the book. I had a schedule set up. The kid didn't even cry all that much. You moms who had a baby with colic? There should be a government program for you where they send over a free nanny and a gift certificate for a night in a hotel. But I tell you, there ain't no such thing as an easy baby. It just means they're like an 8 on the Richter scale as opposed to a 10. I had zero issues, and it was still rough. There was a day when Finn was little and I was so spent that I was crying so hard that my shoulders were moving back and forth, and then I let out this ugly, deep, guttural cry that felt so good. I wondered, *How am I going to do this for eighteen more years?*

I might not be the head of a Fortune 500 company or anything, but up until that point in my life, I could get the hang of most things, so it felt terrible not to be able to bulldog my way through this. It's the newness and it's the hopefulness and it's the feeling like you're constantly screwing it up. Meanwhile, your brain isn't working, and your body's doing weird stuff.

You're holding them all the time, so you do everything with other parts of your body. You're opening stuff with your mouth, stirring with your mouth, crying with your mouth. But you push on and think, *I can do this. This is motherhood. This is the dream, right?* We all worry about what everyone might think if we don't totally have it pulled together. Well, I don't have it together. Still. Not even a little bit. We *just* got Eleanor's birth certificate, and she's five.

It can be easy to sit back and judge, but press PAUSE before you comment. I recently saw a post from a woman who took a picture of a mom at an airport. The mom had her baby on the floor, on a blanket, while she looked at her phone. The world erupted with judgment: "How awful! She is letting her baby lie on the ground!" I looked at that picture and I could tell she was traveling by herself, exhausted, and taking a break. *Back off, folks. She's doing her best.* I get it because I've done it. If there's not a tiger lurking around, why not?

Then a little time goes by and those baby days are over, and there's a shift in difficulty. The twist is that you will miss those days.

I certainly do. I have such baby love and toddler love. I think back to my children being that age, and it crushes me because I won't ever see them again like that. I know they're the same people and all, but those kids, those little leechy babies, they're goners. I see pictures of them and I think, *This little person is not here anymore.* It feels like I've lost them. It's so messed up. They're growing and that's great and natural and good, but damn, I know less about their lives every day. Finn, who used to be my darling little fat meatball, is now all muscles. He looks like he teaches hot yoga. When I look at him, I see less of the baby he was and more of the young man he will become. I can picture him in high school, but I can't quite remember what he looked like in preschool. My heart leaps for joy and breaks down into hysterics at the same time.

Then there's Eleanor. We went through a lot together when she was little, particularly 110 days of bed rest. We had an undeniable bond. She would only let *me* hold her until she was around one, and now she is heading into elementary school. She's funny—like really funny—and she knows it. Sometimes she uses it as a defense mechanism (takes one to know one). We were recently at a park playdate to meet new kindergartners, and Eleanor was incredibly shy. She started talking like an alien and doing bits. It was funny, yes, but I worry about her leaning on that crutch too hard. I knelt down and said, "Eleanor, I know why you want to be funny right now, but you can just be you and that is enough." She teared up and said, "Okay, Mommy." Then I quickly walked away and watched her play while my stomach felt like I'd been in a bar fight.

When I think about them growing up, I get all weepy, and suddenly I'm kissing them too much, and I'm hugging them all the time, and they are like, *What is going on?*

There was this one time with Eleanor at the end of a long day. I'd spent two hours in traffic on the dreaded 101, feeling frustrated about my career and yearning for an easier way of life that I'm sure existed somewhere other than Los Angeles. When I got home, I just picked Eleanor up and held her head and stroked her soft cheek, thinking about how fast this time is whizzing by, and she said through a smirk, "Mommy, are you doing that thing again where you're thinking of me as a baby?"

I was like, "You *are* my baby." And she said, "I'm not a baby. I'm a big girl," and I said, "*I know!* Why do you think I'm losing it?"

I need some therapy and probably a pharmaceutical, or a few.

The cruel trick of it all is that the more independent you make them, the more you know you're doing a good job. But the more independent they are, the less you get of all that you are aching for. We moms are out there, doing our best to make a well-adjusted, kind, independent, brave person, all the while knowing that means they're going to leave us. I asked my son, "Do you think it would be okay if Mommy came to college with you?" He looked at me, and I thought for sure he'd be like, "Yeah, Mommy, we can live together. We'll do Legos all night long." I was planning to play along because it feels so good to pretend. But then he goes, "No, Mommy can't live with me because my girlfriend is gonna come over and I'm gonna hang out with my friends." Hold the phone. Who is she? I already don't like her.

You just hope they remember all of this. Maybe not every day, but the general atmosphere of love. I want them to remember our endless dance parties in the living room, or how we refer to ourselves as Team Sweeney. I hope they remember that we said our prayers at night to remind ourselves of what we are grateful for and what we need to work on to be better people. I want them to remember every single trip we took to Disney because annual passes are really flipping expensive, and I want them to remember me hugging, kissing, squeezing, and tickling them so they never question or doubt how deeply I loved them. Please let them remember all the good. I'll be so pissed if all they remember is me yelling at them to flush the damn toilet.

There are shitty things, exhausting things, frustrating things, but there are also great friends going through the same stuff, and you have to lean into them. It's the only way to get through these times because you know they feel the same way. Get together, cry, drink wine, talk about something that makes you feel good. I can't tell you how many times I've called Jen since becoming a mom, and she's said, "You wanna come over? My house is a mess. I have some leftovers. Bring some cheese."

JEN

Of course my house is a mess. I have no time to do the deep cleaning I fantasize about in bed at night. For some people, it's Ryan Gosling. For me, it's a good steam cleaning.

If you have work-life balance, somebody hates you. Things are pretty balanced in my life in that no one is getting everything they need from me, so it's short sticks all the way around. But other than suddenly realizing I drunkenly bought some stock that did surprisingly well so I can hire the same amount of "help" as a B-list celebrity, I don't see how not to be busy every single moment of every single day. And I set the bar low. As long as the kids are not licking the floor, I'm okay. But sometimes they're licking the floor because I didn't catch them in time and they love to put the most disgusting things in their mouths. I'm convinced that one of these days my son, just to torture me, will be in a truck stop bathroom and find a piece of gum under the sink and put that sucker right in his mouth.

My list of stuff that needs to get done isn't even a list anymore. It's a dossier. And it never gets any shorter. It took me five years to get to the optometrist. Guess what? I need glasses. I need to hose out my car because right now it looks like an opossum family lives in it. It's littered with blankets, stain sticks, fast food bags, and makeup remover (I do my makeup in the car a lot because the kids are restrained in there), but I will never get around to it because I spend the time I am not working picking raisins out of bodily holes that are not mouths and answering questions like "What's the thing my sister pees out of called?" and "Why do I have to wear pants?" and "How come no one wants to see my poop maker?" It is very hard to answer those questions and schedule a mammogram at the same time.

There is just so much to keep track of. Every time one of my children brings home a piece of paper from school, my reaction is "Oh, no, what am I not doing for my kids now?" I'm actually relieved when it's an "ouch report" versus a "Please include a *healthy* beverage with their lunch, you failure of a parent" type of note.

If they don't email me the preschool calendar each month, I don't know what's going on. A three-and-a-half-year-old isn't good at communicating what the plan is for the week, you know? I'll ask, "What did you eat at school today?" and he'll say, "Fire, unicorn, beans." And I'll know he's lying about the beans. We missed Pajama Day, Crazy Hair Day, and Backwards Day. Nobody noticed, though, because they never brush their hair and they wear pajamas backwards pretty much every day anyway.

I went in for orientation before preschool started, and they gave us an information packet. Actually, it was more like a handbook. The teacher said, "Here's a quick list of a couple of things your child will need for the year." It was three pages long. I just assumed they had gone the long-winded route and listed:

Blue Crayon
Red Crayon
Green Crayon, etc.

Nope. It was a legitimate school supply / earthquake emergency / apocalypse list of needs.

I should have read the whole packet. For the first few weeks,

I didn't send Dash to school with a lunch. I thought they said that it was up to the parents to provide a snack and they would provide lunch. Now that I type that, I see how it sounds wrong, but at the time I thought, *Score! All I have to do is slide some Pirate's Booty in his bookbag? Check.* After a month of my son eating only salty snacks, they finally told my husband at pickup, "So, Goldfish? Not enough for a lunch. Maybe try a sandwich? Some baby carrots?"

Honestly, until I became a parent, cheerleading camp was the most grueling thing I'd ever done in my life, so parenting really came as a shock to me. I just read a study that said that being a mom is the equivalent of having two and a half full-time jobs. That sounds about right. I'm so tired and distracted all the time that I call my husband by the kids' names, call my kids by the dog's name, and forget my own name when they ask me at Starbucks. I should just say "Mom," since I hear that about thirty times an hour.

I am tired all day long, starting with the moment I wake up. There should be a series of warning signs next to my bed: Do not stand within five feet of breath. Do not poke with morning boner. Do not ask for things before coffee has been consumed. Do not say that you need to bring _____ with you to school today.

After I'm caffeinated, I rotate my time between wiping things, peeling stickers off things, buckling things, cutting up hot dogs, asking, "Do you need to go potty?," making threats, apologizing for making threats, and yawning.

From about 3:00 on, the mantra in my house is "Survive until bedtime." From the moment the kids are home, it's "Mommy,

I'm bored. Books are boring. TV is boring. Toys are boring. The car is boring. Grandma is boring. The zoo is boring. Fireworks are boring. You're boring." So I tell them to go play outside, and then it's "Mommy, I want to play outside in the water and then come in and put clean clothes on, and then go out and play in the water and then come in and put clean clothes on." Why can't they develop an interest in something I enjoy, like competitive house cleaning or endurance napping?

I have to lie to them just to survive. They think the TV and iPad are constantly broken. They think Disneyland is only open a few days every few years. One time, I told Dash we had to leave the park because it was about to rain, and this kid heard and told her mom, and her mom said, "No, it's not. There's not a cloud in the sky." WTF, lady? Help a sister out.

For some reason, my boy gets especially crazy at about 5:00 to 6:00 p.m. He just has so much energy. Like me when I used to take these green tea diet pills. Dash gets these shark eyes, and he's so fired up it's like he sees your face as a giant soccer ball and just attacks. For the longest time I thought, *Uh-oh, I should be worried about this, right?* But other moms confirmed: "Nope, that's just boys. You just have to wear them out. Get a trampoline." My husband will wrestle our son for forty-five minutes some nights, which I have to commend him for. He gets the crap beaten out of him, my husband does. His glasses have been bent at the hinges since the day he got them.

Then finally, praise the lord, it's nighttime. I consider it a personal success after a long day if I can commit to the bath schedule that I put in place. Some days, I just smell the top of their head and if it isn't too bad, I will use the excess toothpaste around their mouth to clean the bottom half of their face, then we put on clean undies and call it good. When we just had one kid, it was dinner, bath, jammies, teeth, cuddles, five to ten books, prayers, songs, and then to bed. Now that we have two, we get pizza delivered, yell at everyone to clean up their stuff, go around and pick up random articles of clothing strewn all over the house, try to avoid looking in the kitchen sink, wrestle them into something that kind of looks like pajamas, lie on the floor holding a book while getting jumped on, rake toys into a pile, put the kids in bed, and pour wine.

I spend the first half hour or so after they go to bed just trying to get the house back in order so I'm not starting behind the eight ball the next day. It would be one thing if they were showering love and praise on me for killing myself to get things done, but that's not really their thing. One day, I was driving my kids home from soccer and Dash said, "I don't like you, and I never have, and when we get out of the car, I'm going to kick you." I held it together, and then we got out of the car and sure enough, he closed the door and kicked me. Gotta hand it to him. The kid has follow-through.

But I know I have it pretty darn #blessed, even on my hardest days. I know it's not a competition, but sometimes I think about how much harder some other parents have it. My mom was doing it mostly solo, like millions of other moms out there. I don't even like trying to put the duvet cover on by myself. I can't imagine how overwhelming it is to be a single parent or the parent of a kid who has even greater needs than mine do.

I have just one cousin, Austin. He was born with some major difficulties, and my aunt and uncle adopted him as a baby knowing there would be some challenges in caring for him. That's because they are saintlike people. Austin has severe autism and intellectual disabilities and also one of the best senses of humor I've ever encountered. I remember being super young and looking at his bad eye, and his good one, which was not much better, and feeling that I needed to take extra care with him. He filled both my brother and me with pure joy. He laughed loudly and could burp even louder, on command. That makes you a general among the ranks of children. He was older than both my brother and me, but we reminded him to put on his coat before going outside to play and not to lift the huge Kirby vacuum cleaner over his head, no matter how impressive a bit it was. He is, developmentally, still the same as he was when we were kids, only he moves a little more slowly, as we all do. But he still loves vacuum cleaners.

I compare my aunt's and uncle's patience during long days with how inept I am at dealing with the post office being closed, my confusion at how to work multiple TV remotes, and how annoyed I get that there are currently googly eyes stuck all over my kitchen floor. I clearly am not equipped to handle the life they chose, and I am humbled by their commitment and love. Because this thing we signed on for is a huge bleeping commitment.

We're all just trying to get it right. We know a million things will go wrong, but we keep trying, hoping that the love filters through. We all have our own way of showing it. I look at Kristin and I see how she is so good at play—she comes up with these games out of nowhere—and you can see the kids love her for it. She's fine with letting the dishes sit in the sink so she can make time for tickling. She's the best tickler. I suck at tickling, but I can cuddle until the cows come home. I will stop doing anything, be late for anything, neglect any adult chore in order to cuddle my babies. And at least for now, they love it too. I tell them that if they ever stop hugging me I will sell them to the circus. I'm positive it's terrible parenting, but I really like cuddles.

Maybe your expression of love is a perfect lunch every day. Maybe it's teaching your kids soccer. For me, making sure the house is super clean (moderately livable) is one way of showing my kids I care about their environment. I make a point to listen to their ideas and feelings too. That's really important to me. I want them to know that no matter how truly insane they're being, I will listen and help them solve their problems without judgment. Whatever that thing is, you make time for it in the crushing rush of stuff you have to get through every day.

The last time my brother visited, we were all up past bedtime, and I was lamenting the terrible job I was doing as a parent. We decided to burn off some of the kids' overtired sillies with a disco dance party. As I twerked and jiggled with them, my brother said, "This is what they'll remember about your parenting. Not that you were inconsistent about bedtimes. That you danced with them. I hope they always remember this." I hope I do too.

To me, motherhood is one big case of Stockholm syndrome. They make you so crazy all day that you cry, and then they give you a hug and it makes you cry some more. But at the end of your hardest days, you look on your phone at pictures of your kid and you set a reminder not to take all you've got for granted.

I KEEP FOOLS ALIVE SO HARD

Before you have kids, you know some things are gonna be hard: the birth, the tantrums, paying for college. What you'd never guess is that somehow the hardest thing is something you've taken for granted your entire life—the simple act of eating. It doesn't sound difficult: when we were growing up, we ate what was put in front of us, or we didn't eat. For lunch, our moms packed us a bologna and cheese sandwich and some Doritos, and we were *psyched*. Yes, our corpses will survive doomsday because we are comprised of 98 percent additives and preservatives, but making a school lunch was not a two-hour ordeal. Now, you need the compartment thing and the sandwich press thing. Moms are packing tins full of broccoli matchsticks and tiny cheeses and lunches where the food has been cut up and styled to look like sushi. We'll try anything to con kids into eating something remotely healthy. But guess

#IMOMSOHARD

what? You're going to go to great lengths, and they aren't going to eat it anyway.

When you've got a picky eater, you're making nine meals a day because everyone has different needs. It's such torture that eventually, you give up after like an hour and a half of trying to get them to eat something, anything—seriously, anything—and you say, "That's it, you're going to bed hungry." And then a half hour later when you're trying to watch Netflix, a voice calls out, "Mom, I'm *sooooo* hungry." And you get up and make them peanut butter and jelly or give them Goldfish. They win. They are tiny and have no actual power, but they are like tiny Roman conquering soldiers, and they are winning this war.

JEN

I used to be a pretty good cook, but now I make three things: veggie lasagna, mac and cheese, and grilled chicken—which my husband actually makes. Okay, sometimes I also buy Trader Joe's Chinese food and add stuff to it to make it even less healthy. Like butter. Lots of butter.

The hilarious thing (hilarious in a "the universe is a cruel and uncaring place" way) is that it really doesn't matter what I make. My kids don't eat it. I know a lot of parents who say, "They eat what I eat or they go hungry." Really? I make what they'll eat or I'll go crazy. We've all learned to love chicken nuggets. People will tell you, "If they're hungry, they'll eat." You need to meet my son. My son is so stubborn, he would go skeletal in a week if I tried to get him to eat some spinach.

In the glorious first two years of Dash's life, I was a childhood nutrition champ. I did all the research on superfoods. I made an almond milk berry concoction with quinoa, and he drank fruit shakes in a BPA-free sippy cup. I made him eat his colors, he had a balanced diet of protein, plants, and carbs, and oh yeah, everything was organic.

You know who's really smart? The person who put "organic" on everything. We'll buy anything with that stamp because it instantly relieves the mom guilt. We're like, yeah, it's apple juice, but it's *organic*. Hot dogs? Organic. Jelly beans? Organic! But it's expensive, which I resent. I can't justify ever getting a manicure when spending $2 more on milk will keep my daughter from needing a bra when she's in second grade, and now my nails look like shit.

So okay, for those first two years, we were all avocados and kale. Then Dash turned two and he was like, *Shut. It. Down.* I don't know what happened. I followed all the advice. I made a big, wonderful variety of foods, I presented things five times, I went for a real cool no-presh atmosphere at the table, but my boy is a master negotiator in that there was *no negotiation*. He hadn't even been on the planet for three full years, but he made it clear that when it came to dinner, he was the captain now. But not like Jean-Luc Picard, like Ahab: obsessive, angry, and willing to go down with the ship.

These days, Dash screams like I'm beating him if I put mango on his plate. I'm constantly saying, "Just try it." I have literally begged my kids to take *one* bite. It's not like he's resisting for kicks once in a blue moon. It's every day, twenty times a day, that I plead with him to eat one damn spoonful. I'm not serving them Scotch bonnets or octopus sashimi. It's maybe . . . a green bean. Green beans literally have zero flavor on their own, and the way I cook them they are smothered in cream sauce and fried onions so they are GD delicious. But no. Not one morsel of a green thing will make it across his lips. So I've given up on green and have moved on to the dreaded white foods—white rice, white bread, white pasta—but even those are a hard pass. It's gotten so bad that there have been times when I've begged my son to please eat Cheetos and maybe some M&M's.

Meanwhile, thirty minutes after he's walked away from the table I'll find him eating tissue paper in the corner, and I'll think, *Well, it's got to have* something *in it. It's basically roughage.* I have googled the chemical makeup of typing paper, just hoping there's something good in it. I can't get him to eat real food, but he'll saunter outside to eat poison berries and wood chips. I don't know what his deal is. I mean, I didn't put a dead puppy on his plate. It's called ravioli. Why all the screaming? And then one random day he'll eat four full bowls of oatmeal.

It must be karma. When I was little, I ate nothing. My mom would get so desperate that she'd just hand me a bowl of frosting to eat, which I used to think was bad parenting, but now I get it.

I think I just had a general aversion to food. Now that's entirely gone away, and I don't really have an aversion to anything but mushrooms (and there are some olives I'm not really that into). Mostly I've become a human trash compactor. I never want to throw anything away, so for lunch, I'm eating a salad with dried bananas on it. Do you know why you have never seen a salad with dried bananas on it on a café menu? Because it is disgusting. But I have to eat it or it will go to waste.

I joke about how hard it is to feed the kids, but you guys, I do actually worry. Feeding your kids is the one thing you can't slack on. You can never ever forget for a moment that you're a mother until your kids can feed themselves. It's like there's an alarm bell that goes off three times a day, and if you don't run and push the button before the timer goes off, everything explodes. No matter where you are, you have to stop what you're doing and make sure to give life-sustaining sustenance to the creatures you made. I mean, it's not a big whoop if you forget to brush their teeth every now and again, or if you send them to school without socks. But if you don't feed your kids, they can literally be taken away from you. It's our job as parents to keep these tiny people alive, so I took my son to the pediatrician to make sure that I wasn't failing at that, and she told me to relax and lay off a little. The kid will survive. There are calories going in. He's not going to die today.

So now, if I can get him to eat a ketchup packet or a fun-size Snickers, I feel like a hero. *Yes! Calories in!*

I guess it could be worse. I could have one of those kids who only eat super fancy foods, like a kid who is precociously obsessed with Gordon Ramsay or drinks made with shrub. I'm off the hook for high-maintenance cooking. And forget that "too many cooks in the kitchen" thing—when there are too many kids in the kitchen, cooking is straight-up dangerous. I could still kind of cook when I only had one kid, but with two? Forget it. You have to make things that are really forgiving. At dinner,

I'll send my husband out to grill some chicken, and I'll tell my-self, *You just need to focus on these brussels sprouts.* Then, at the critical moment when they're crispy and perfect and ready to take out, my Spidey sense tingles and I turn around to see that my son is about to jump off the couch into a closed window. So I have to go put out that fire. And then I come back and find that the brussels sprouts are literally on fire. I've had nights where everything's burning because the youngest is so hungry that she started eating dog food out of the dog's bowl and the dog's pissed, so I have to turn my attention away from the stove to make sure we don't go to the ER for a dog bite. I have gotten so good at burning dinner since I had two kids that I can burn the main course and two sides in the last thirty seconds of cook time.

The thing is, I actually like to cook. It's not just that I'm a masochist, or even that I want my family to eat (though I do want that—lord, do I want that). I also want them to know that I care about them, that I care about what makes them happy. If my kids would just tell me, "Listen, Mom, if you could put together a quick meatloaf and some mashed potatoes, we'd eat that," I'd butcher the cow and grind the beef myself—and I'm pretty much a vegetarian.

What I actually like to make is Nebraska food, the kind my grandmother used to cook. She could clean out the fridge, scrape the bottom, fry it up in the bacon grease she kept on top of the stove in an Avon container, and it would be delicious. The main ingredients in most of my dishes are cream cheese, sour cream, a can of soup, salt, pepper, and cheese. I'm pretty

sure if those were the only ingredients, it would still be amazing. That combo is how I get my husband to eat broccoli: just
float a stem in that mixture. Hey, float a turd in that mixture
and anybody would eat it. He told me I should write a cookbook
called *The Nebraska Palette: Beige and Delicious.* The state vegetable is corn, and that's not even a real vegetable, you guys.
That's corn. It's no surprise that my two favorite flavors are
salty and crispy.

In Nebraska, we take foods that are already a complete meal
and add them to other foods to make a dish. You take a can
of soup that's already done and condensed, and then you add
another processed food, and then you put Tater Tots on top of
it, and then you bake it at 350° for forty-five minutes. I dare
you not to love it. You add Tater Tots to anything and it's good.
Who's ever had a bad Tater Tot? I'd eat those things frozen.

When you go to a party in Nebraska, you're going to have
the three Cs: a coozie, a casserole, and a Crock-Pot. There's
probably potato-chicken casserole, tuna casserole, and at least
one green bean casserole at every gathering. To make a good
casserole, you simply grab any kind of packet you can get in the
dressing aisle, add it to a Crock-Pot of random delicious stuff,
and people love it. If there isn't bubbling melted cheese pooling
on the top of it, I don't want it.

What can I say—I'm a product of where I'm from. I want
cornflakes on top of potatoes. I want a breakfast that's a serving
of casserole, a full pastry, and something topped with jam. I
want a dip that is so heavy it hurts my wrists when I carry it. I
want a dip that needs to be reheated throughout the day so you

137

can get a chip into it. I want my appetizer plate to snap in half. I want to bring a side dish to a potluck that my husband has to carry from the car. I want a dessert made from a combination of other complete desserts.

Even though she's also from Nebraska, Kristin is a healthy eater. I don't know how she does it. She makes salmon, salads, and roasted stuff. I know she's always saying to herself before she comes over to my house for dinner, *Please let there be one thing that doesn't have bacon in it*. Hey, at least the bacon is organic. Kristin, can you please be the person in my life who likes to eat what I make, even if you have to lie? Pleeeeease?

KRISTIN

Yeah, I'm a healthy eater until I hang out with Jen and she says, "Do you want to get spinach artichoke dip?" I auto-reply, "Yes. Yes, I do." That kind of thing was all I ate when I was growing up. It was a healthy choice of pizza, hamburgers, or a casserole. There was one time I ate some vegetables when someone offered me a dollar to eat this carrot/raisin/mayonnaise combo. But this other kid ate a cricket for $5, so I'm feeling pretty good about my choice.

I will drink the occasional smoothie now and again, but unlike Jen, I do not cherish time spent in the kitchen. If I could pull a lever and have a healthy, balanced meal on the table for my family, I would do it in a second. I genuinely want my kids to learn to love eating nature's glorious bounty, but *there is no lever.* There are just hours and hours of planning, shopping, prepping, cooking, and cleaning. So instead of the wonders of nature, I find myself embracing the wonders of takeout, ordering in, eating out, and meal delivery.

It would be easier to be more like a paler, thicker Giada De Laurentiis if my kids would get on board. With my kids, they only like a food maybe two days of the week, but you never know which days. One kid will like chicken tenders on Monday and Wednesday, and the other on Tuesday and Thursday, so you're always going to have one who's unhappy.

I understand that my kids don't like to eat anything new. I can get behind that. I will order a burger at every restaurant I go to because I don't like change. But it's like their taste buds transform completely every eight hours. I tell them, "But you ate this yesterday and loved it. Why don't you eat it now?" And they'll say, "Because it tastes different at night."

If I'm honest, though, even before kids, I wasn't the greatest cook. When I go to a friend's for dinner, what I bring probably has a price tag on it. When Jen hosts a dinner, there's so much going on that her place looks like mission control at NASA. She's one of those cooks who make it seem easy. I take one look at all the dishes and delicious things flying around and I proclaim, "I'll bartend. For myself primarily."

I know there are people who find joy and relaxation in the kitchen, but I am just not one of them. I'd rather color or work with plants. I have a friend named Lynn who has four boys who are like four minutes apart in age. When you go over to her house, it's a tumbleweed of basketball shorts and tighty-whities rolling around, and she's in the middle of it, just chillin'. I was at her place one afternoon, and she just started pulling stuff out

139

of cabinets. She put egg noodles and chicken and cream sauce in a Crock-Pot. She tossed in some green beans, and turned that sucker on. I leaned over the pot, salivating, and asked her, "What is *that*?" And she said, "I don't know, just some chicken." It was like an accidental casserole. That's what drives me crazy about people who can cook. They just assume everyone else can do it. They're like, "It's easy, just throw in this and this." I promise you I've screwed up something that only has two ingredients, so yeah, I've been known to stop by the occasional drive-through (three times a week is occasional, right?). It's a survival tactic. Your life is just so damn busy when you're a mom. It's impossible to keep up with the relentless food making.

And yet, they need food. I mean, they cannot survive without it. I don't know where their energy comes from. They are on the move all day, every day. Kids never do anything without running to it. They'll go to pick a book off a shelf like it's a fifty-yard dash. They burn about five thousand calories a day. I want to do a Fitbit challenge and put mine on Finn. I'd crush it. He'd have thirty-five thousand steps before school even started.

The point is, I would love to be a mom who cooks every night even if I do suck at it, because isn't that what everyone tells us would be best for them? I get a stab of guilt every time I let something pass their lips that I didn't make myself. But I pick up the kids at 5:30, I get home at 5:50, and then what? I'm supposed to chop broccoli for forty-five minutes? I wouldn't even get to see their faces. I'd way rather play some Go Fish than bake fish sticks. So hello, El Pollo drive-through. I'm there so much that I pull up to the speaker and a familiar voice says, "Hey, Kristin. The usual?"

"Yes, Angie. Thank you. Tell your family hello."

The tricky thing about the takeout cheat is that I do want to instill good habits with my kids. I don't want them to struggle later in life. When I was growing up in Nebraska, we didn't have many options for fast food. My mom cooked every night. She wasn't setting the world on fire with her meals, but the meat and veggies were fresh, and we didn't eat a lot of junk food. My husband's dad died of heart disease. I'm not going to speak ill of the dead, and since I never met him myself it's a tough thing to think, but something in me shifted when my daughter said, "I wish I could have met Dead Grandpa Greg, but he died because he ate too many cheeseburgers." She's not wrong. And then I realized how much Dead Grandpa Greg is missing out on because of the food he ate, and I started to make some changes in our diet. Look, I'm not a health nut, but I don't want the kids to be on a first-name basis with Burger King. I'm trying to serve them healthy foods. There's a little part of me that sees every meal as a chance to help them out down the road so that they're able to develop enough sense to say, "Yeah, the Bloomin' Onion sounds good, but I think I'll have the beet salad instead, thanks."

That's why I put so much effort into making the kids' lunches. I don't have time to crank out homemade pasta, but I've got the time to curate an A+ lunch. My kids' school does not have hot lunch, so I pack lunches every school day. When I make their lunch, I always try to imagine them going camping instead of being at school, so my philosophy is to put in a little good, a little bad—something for fuel and something for fun.

However, I will say the lunches I make vary wildly depending on how long it has been since we've been to the grocery store. Right after I've shopped, it's freshly cut fruit, raisins, hard-boiled eggs, carrots with ranch, turkey roll-ups, and some air-filled fake chips. When we need to go shopping, my kids' lunches are awful. I'll give them frozen lima beans and a sandwich baggie full of panko bread crumbs. Or a lunch where literally every item in there has to be opened with a can opener.

I do occasionally show up at school for a little lunch recon, to look at the other lunches so I can see how I'm doing. I like to casually walk by all the lunches and then nonchalantly grill the kids about their options. "Hey, Hudson, I see you're eating brown rice and veggies. Do you like it, or does your mom pack it for show?" Sometimes I think, *Hey, I'm doing pretty good.* And other times, I'm like, *Seriously? Your kid eats those little tomatoes? Well, good for you.*

The only problem with being the main lunch packer (besides the fact that it's thankless and exhausting) is that kids' lunch food is delicious. I can pound a bag of Pirate's Booty in the time it takes me to make a PB&J. No wonder I can't lose those last few pounds. My afternoon meals are made up of whatever they don't eat at school that day. I'll eat like half a chicken nugget, leftover Scooby-Doo gummies, and a handful of granola, which by the way is not good for you but it costs like $7, so I'm not going to waste it. Sometimes I wonder if I pack their lunches just so I can "clean up" the leftovers. It's like I'm dumpster diving in the comfort of my own home.

God love my husband. He had to pack lunches for a week, and now he has a small idea of how hard it is. His lunches are total train wrecks. He packs them meals that he would like to eat, like fully loaded sandwiches with peperoncini and a bottle of hot sauce. He once put an overripe banana in Eleanor's lunch, and by the time it got home (because of course she didn't eat it) it was black and oozing banana mush. I believe all husbands pack lunches that they would like to eat themselves. I'm waiting for the call that mine sent hot wings and a Sam Adams in my kid's lunchbox.

In the rare event that their lunch bag comes back empty, I think, *Well, that was one good lunch.* I feel like I climbed a mountain when they eat everything in their bag. I'll corner them after school and grill them: "So it was good, right? What was your favorite part?" I talk about it for way too long. I'll be like, "At first, I was going to go with a cheese-meat combo, but at the last minute I jumped in with a chicken wrap. Tough call, but I felt good about it. But what about the kiwi? That was a nice surprise, wasn't it? You thought I was going to give you another apple? But no, boom, kiwi. Superfood. Did you love it?" And they will just look at me and say, "If we say yes, will you let us play on the iPad now?"

It's tough out there, y'all. You're not physically connected to them anymore, feeding them from the belly button or the boob, but you are still responsible for making sure they grow and thrive. It's so easy to feel like you're failing at it when you see what other moms are making on Pinterest, but I think Jen's pediatrician had it right. Calories in. There may not be an adorable rice ball shaped like a panda on my kid's plate, but as long as their plate has nuggets and something veggie-ish on it, I consider that a win.

I HIT THE TOWN
(AND AM IN BED BY 9:30 P.M.)
SO HARD

Every women's magazine contains the same three articles in each issue: (1) "Feel Guilty for Not Eating More Kale!," (2) "Tired? Scientific Breakthrough Says You Should Try Sleeping More!," and (3) "The No-Fail Solution to Any Problem in Your Relationship: DATE NIGHT." As much as we hate to admit it, they may be onto something with that last one. Do you know how hard it is to have a conversation when kids are around? It's like you're on a merry-go-round and your partner is waiting in line and you just get to shout a single unintelligible word every time you pass by. Date night lets you get off the ride for a minute. When you sit down across from your partner, you remember that there was a reason you chose to yoke yourself to them for all eternity. Talking like that is such a good reminder that you're not just a mom. You're also a person and a partner and someone with interests not featured on the Cartoon Network who can use words with more than two syllables. Occasionally. (See?)

Make no mistake, you will still talk mostly about the kids, but once you've had a couple of vodka tonics, it feels like a warm bonding activity that will bring you closer together— *Look what we made!*—instead of like running the triage unit at a level 4 trauma center: *What have we done???*

KRISTIN

My husband and I have tried to go on more dates now that the kids are a little bit older, and the last three ended in an argument and we came home early. Date night feels forced, and nobody can choose a restaurant. Or you do the same ol' same ol', and that makes you feel bad 'cause you wonder, *Are we boring?* It's also hard to just downshift and go on a date. Dating, in general, sucks. Why would it be any better with someone you married? In fact, it's worse now because when he bites down on his fork and can't remember to wear a clean shirt, you can't ghost him—you have to go home with him for eternity. Obviously, time together as a couple is very important, and I love when my husband and I are connecting and having a good time. But mostly that comes with a spontaneous "Hey, wanna grab a beer? Can you see if the babysitter can stay an extra hour?" And then it's just us. And I overlook the fork thing.

Anyway, it had been a while since my husband and I had gone on a date—a real date, you know, where you wear pants and you don't bring the kids along. His birthday was coming up, so I picked up my phone to make a dinner reservation at a grown-up restaurant—the kind where they don't give you crayons but they do give you a separate fork for dessert—when I thought, *Screw it. WE'RE GOING TO VEGAS!* I know, I am the world's most incredible wife! I deserve an award—or at least a decent participation medal.

Just to go away for twenty-six hours, I had to hire an overnight babysitter, pack lunches, prepare two separate "just heat me up" dinners, hire a dog walker, leave car seats, write elaborate instructions for the bedtime routine, list doctors' numbers, clean the house, and buy two new episodes of *Mickey Mouse Clubhouse* and *Henry Danger* on iTunes. And yet, I was still *pumped* about getting away with my husband, just the two of us.

I told my son, who is six, "Mommy and Daddy are going to Las Vegas for Daddy's birthday." He asked, "Why can't we go too?" I told him, "Because they don't let kids into Vegas." He looked at me and said, "Fine. Then I'm not calling you when I go to college." The kid cuts to the quick.

It's not like he hates being around our babysitters. In fact, I think he likes them more than he likes me. I can't blame him. Who wouldn't prefer to be around a Mary Poppins type who sings the day away instead of a bossy grouch who is always threatening to throw out his Legos? But listen, I've got nothing bad to say about babysitters because if I didn't have them, I would die. There are three girls we use on a regular basis, each of them more delightful than the last, and I'm very tight-lipped about them because people like to steal them. (I'm not naming names, but if I were, I would name Jen, Jen, and Jen. And also Jen.)

Okay, it's not entirely true that I have *nothing* bad to say about babysitters. The one big complaint I have is that it's like a million dollars to pay for them. When I was growing up, I was stoked if I got paid in paper money instead of the fifty cents I'd get for helping my elderly neighbor shovel snow from the driveway she didn't even use. I thought, *Oh yeah, I'm going home with a ten dollar bill, y'all! GUESS jeans, I'm coming for you.* For what I'm paying our sitters, I feel like I should come home to kids who are fluent in Cantonese or know how to code. But we're not really paying them for results. We pay our sitters a lot of dough because we want them to be available. We want them to cancel plans when we call.

I actually loved babysitting when I was a teen and even into my twenties. I've always loved being around kids. They're fun and they laugh at my fart jokes. I always said yes when parents asked me to babysit. Except if it was this one family. They were super wealthy but they were also super cheap, and their kid was a real a-hole. One night while I was over there, she angry-pooped in the tub. I had to give her a bath—by the way, I never make my babysitters give baths because no one should have to smell my kids' butts; we're not paying them *that* much—and she sat in the tub, got mad that her parents were gone, and crapped in the bubble bath, and I had to clean it up. They paid me so little that I thought, *Good thing I came with an empty stomach and ate you dummies out of house and home.* Remember, I grew up in Nebraska, where when you went grocery shopping, you bought like you were laying in for winter, not like it was an adorable stop at a European market for a baguette and an apple. I destroyed their stash like a rodent infestation.

I used to love it when my parents went out. They weren't real particular about who they left us with. They pretty much just asked, "Is your daughter over thirteen? She's fine." I can't believe they were so lax about it because I was the biggest tattletale with babysitters. It wasn't like they thought they were leaving me with Mrs. Doubtfire. I had one sitter who you might describe as being from the wrong side of the tracks. She waited about thirty seconds after my parents left for the night to ask me, "Hey, Kristin, is it cool if my boyfriend comes over? Don't tell your mom," and I was like, "Oh, totally," like, *I got your back, girl. I'm cool*. He came over, I saw them making out on the couch from the top of the stairs when I was supposed to be in bed, and then she smoked a cigarette. *What!* I couldn't rat her out fast enough. After she left, the door hadn't even closed before I spit out, "The babysitter had her boyfriend over and she kissed him on the mouth and then she smoked." I said it all in one breath. I would make a terrible member of the Mafia. My mom acted shocked and gasped, "What?!" all pearl-clutchy, but in her head I know she was thinking, *Ugh, but that girl is always available*. I guess it didn't bother my mom that much because that sitter came a few more times, and then she stole a pair of my mom's jeans (which gives a greater moment for pause), and she was gone forever. Smoking and smooching, you got a pass, but stealing was a bridge too far.

I don't worry about any of that stuff with our sitters, which is why I felt okay leaving the kids overnight with Angel (yeah, I know, but it's literally her name) when we were headed to Vegas. After we got in the car to go to the airport, I texted her the twenty-five other things I forgot. I fantasized about how the night would play out. Obviously, I would magically shrink to a size 4, and everywhere I walked there would be a light breeze in my hair. We'd walk down the Strip, and people would make way for us whenever we got to a table because they would be able to tell that this was a Big Night Out and we were going to make it count.

I had wanted to get to the airport early, have a Bloody Mary, flirt a little with my husband, and then casually walk to our flight. Nope. By the time we actually got to the departures drop-off, we were running so late that my husband looked at me and said, "We gotta run." I locked eyes with him and said, "I run a healthy nine and a half minute mile. I got this."

So we huffed and puffed to Gate 46, where we barely made our flight. It was totally worth the brush with cardiac arrest. Once we got on that plane, it was heaven. For the rest of the trip, we talked. To each other. Uninterrupted. Talking with my husband, when there isn't a shitty tone coming from either one of us, is my favorite thing. We love to talk about movies, TV shows, plot points, and characters, and then add in what we would've done or something ridiculous. We also love to make an escape plan for a zombie apocalypse.

My husband lives to give me a hard time. It's his favorite thing. And mine too. He imitates me and makes fun of my lisp—but I know he actually likes it. When we were dating, he said my voice was darling. The playful teasing and disaster planning usually end in a pretend fight because he hesitates before saying I'd be his first choice on a survival team. Up yours, buddy. I'll go find a zombie apocalypse survival team full of firefighters and hot lifeguards, and then I won't let you on our team. But I digress.

We got a room in the Venetian. It had not one, but two queen beds. It was perfect. Ah, the two-bed solution. Hump in one and sleep in the other. Or hump in one and he can have that one. Plus, it had a huge bathtub. I've never been so clean. As I mentioned, it was his birthday so we fooled around for about eight minutes, which is a marathon for us. When my husband and I have a sexual encounter that lasts more than six minutes, he refers to it as R&B sex. And then we ate a leftover meatball sub in bed for lunch. That's true love, when you feel comfortable enough with a person that you can relax and eat a real sloppy sandwich.

We spent the day doing nothing and everything. When you are married and especially as parents, you spend every weekend doing something or going somewhere: birthday parties, soccer, basketball, karate, dance—and that's just Saturday. You crave a day to do nothing. Nothing is wonderful. So we didn't do anything. We sauntered. We ate breakfast and read a newspaper. We walked around and talked about Elvis Presley and close magic. We sat by a pool even though it was a little chilly because we could. We did nothing, and it was everything.

We were in bed by 10:00 p.m. and up at 7:00 a.m., when everyone else in Vegas is just rolling back to their rooms. We walked around the city. I had ten thousand steps on my Fitbit by 11:00 a.m. And it felt so good to just stroll. I can't tell you the last time I walked without the intention of getting somewhere fast. We got to listen to music that didn't try to teach us anything about the solar system or good dental care.

On the way back, I didn't care that our flight was delayed three times because my husband and I just chilled with each other. The whole date reminded me why I had let this guy knock me up in the first place. Listen, if you have a baby with someone, you are connected forever whether you want to be or not, so you better choose a good one to be in the bunker with. And I think I did.

When we got home, Angel looked so beat that I'm sure she won't miss a pill for the next seven years.

JEN

Sitters love Kristin because when they come over, she's wait-ing at the door for them to arrive, and then as soon as they're inside, she's like, "Hi! Okay, here's the kids. Bye!" I, on the other hand, welcome them into my home for a brief orientation before the evening gets underway. I'm like, "There are just a few things I'd like to go over before we leave. Please be seated. Let me just cue up this PowerPoint deck, and we'll get started. Number one, do not use the stove. Number two, the bathroom. The toilet is one of those European flush toilets, so you might have to hold down the handle a little longer. You can have any food that you want. Ah, yes, the microwave. Did I show you where it is? Our TV is a little bit tricky. You've got to use this remote to turn it on and then this one to change channels . . ." Then after an hour or so, I finally get out the door, and five minutes later I text to ask, "Could you just take a quick picture of the kids and send it to me? Okay. Thanks. And maybe another one in ten minutes?"

We almost never do sitters. We didn't hire one for the first third of each of my kids' lives. I feel like I need to have a really good reason to get one. I don't want to cheap out when it comes to the safety of our kids, but it's like $15 to $20—*an hour.* American dollars. Cash money. People talk about unemployment in this country, and how we have to raise the minimum wage, but there is a clear solution: let's just hire everyone who needs a job as a babysitter. Two birds, one stone.

I will confess that we used to interview and screen our sitters. Nothing too intense. I'd just ask for their references, experience, and access to all of their social media passwords. When I was a kid, my mom would just drop me off at the military base nursery where they put a piece of masking tape across our backs with our name on it to keep us all straight. There'd be one sitter and like thirteen kids. I wish I could be that chill about leaving my kids with someone, but I get nervous sometimes with sitters. I mean, I do a good once-over when I hand my keys to a valet. You think I'm going to let my kids stay with just anyone? It's a leap of faith. But I think people are mostly good. When I get anxious, I try to remind myself that you've got to put a little trust in the universe. Besides, there are strict state and federal laws overseeing the treatment of children. And I have a nanny cam and ask my neighbor to snoop. I'll even make threats. But as long as that fifteen-year-old has great references, CPR training, a high GPA, no boyfriend, and a desire to make $15 an hour, I'll give her a try.

I have never been accused of being an optimist; I consider myself a realist. I like to prepare for the worst but *hope* for the best. Especially in other people, I can see the silver lining. (I currently prefer a rose-gold or platinum lining, but I'll take anything shiny.)

I may also be overcompensating by having high standards for who will take care of my kids since I was fired from the only two babysitting jobs I ever had: one night in December 1990 and one in January 1991. I want to feel like there's a real high bar to have what it takes to be a successful babysitter.

It sure as hell felt that way to me. The first time I got fired, it was for eating too many fruit roll-ups. I had arrived hungry and I wanted to do a good job, so I ate three roll-ups to keep my blood sugar up. (Okay, it may have been a *box* or two. I was just being cautious.) I was so scared of doing something wrong. Now that there's iPhones, and parents have every movie channel, it's pretty cush to babysit, but I just sat in the living room with no lights or TV on, listening to the clock tick and trying to figure out why their house smelled weird—like cat pee, shrimp, and anger and resentment. That was the latest 9:30 I've ever seen.

When I finally went back into the kitchen to throw away my wrappers I noticed that they were one of those families that washed out and hung their Ziploc bags to dry so that they could reuse them. I had a feeling that didn't bode well for a generous "go nuts with the fruit roll-ups" policy. I was right. When she got home, the mother called my mom to snitch. I think she expected that my mom would say, "Thank you so much for letting me know. I will handle this right away and with vigor." But my mom was having none of it. She was like, "My daughter was hungry, and you didn't feed her? What kind of monster are you?" I never got called again.

The other time I babysat, it was for a three-month-old. I was maybe twelve. I hadn't totally mastered riding a bike without training wheels. I don't know what that mom was smoking that she would trust me with an infant. I barely trusted myself with our kids at three months. I didn't leave my husband alone with our kids until they were two. I had to ask my mom, "Mom, can I babysit for a baby?" She thought it over and was like, "Yeah, all you have to do is give her a bottle and make sure she doesn't sit around in a wet diaper," so that's what was in my head as I was saying goodbye to these parents. I just kept giving the baby a new bottle and diaper every fifteen minutes. The mom came home an hour and a half later and said, "You changed her *five* times?" I think she did the math and figured out it would be cheaper to hire a more experienced sitter who would not lay waste to her diaper supply. End of gig.

I've never had to fire a sitter because we only hire people who come very highly recommended (because they used to work for Kristin). But I know I'm being overly precious about who I leave my kids with. Kids are resilient. And it's good for them to have experiences outside of the sweet, sweet bubble of just you and the rest of your family because that's how they learn—or at the very least, how they develop a strong appreciation for what they've got going. You're teaching them that the world is a safe place, that people can be trusted. I hate the idea that my kids will grow up suspicious of everyone they meet. We spend so much time worrying. It's nice to take a break from imagining the five hundred terrible things that could happen with a barbecue skewer if you aren't there to prevent them. Every time you come home to a house full of sleeping kids, it's more evidence that life is not a catastrophe.

All I really want in a babysitter is someone who will keep them alive and not drink my wine—not the good stuff, anyway.

I'm leaving them with kids who are already in bed 90 percent of the time. I just need someone to let me know if my daughter is shooting vomit in her bed or if the house is on fire. If there's a fire, I want to feel confident that she'll grab them and take them to the neighbor's house—or at least outside on the porch. Otherwise, she can just stare at her phone or enjoy my full cable package for a couple of hours while I pay her the equivalent of what I would pay a master plumber to remodel my powder room. Why is it so hard to find someone to do this? If someone offered me that job, I'd take it in a heartbeat. Get paid to sit on the couch and catch up on *Game of Thrones*? Twist my arm.

We have managed to have *a few* nights out after having children. And I mean a few. Really not many. I would like to do more, but my husband . . . yeah, there's no punch line. He just doesn't want to go out on dates as much as I do—like a guy who's just not into belts or fancy jeans. It's just not his jam. It's not a sob story—he loves me. I know this. But this is one thing we disagree on (the other thing is chunky or creamy peanut butter). I'd like to leave the house more; him, not so much.

If it's my birthday or our anniversary, sure, he'll usually take me out, but we dated for such a long time before we got married and had kids that it was like we had had one long date night. He took me to really nice places and always paid. He took us on fun vacations. It was a blast. And then we had our wedding and he was like, "Okay, that will be all." Coincidentally, this was right around the time when I stopped going to the gym.

I talk a big game about how I'd love to go out more, but really, staying in is where it's at most of the time. A lot of it is that our kids are so young and we're so damn tired day and night. Someday, we'll get back to date night. Right now, food delivery, comfy pants, and crappy TV sound so much easier. And cheaper.

Is this lame? My big romantic idea for how I want us to spend time together these days is to listen to podcasts. Like how people used to listen to radio shows at night. I'm a sucker for a shared listening experience. We had this cool old 1970s console I found on Craigslist that I made my husband pick up one Thanksgiving Day for $50. The irony is that some other wife wanted it *out* of her living room when relatives came and I wanted it *in* mine when relatives came. I liked the mid-century warm wood, but I loved the soothing sound. It had such smooth bass that it almost had an echo to it. It reminded me of listening to music with my parents when I was a little kid. My husband and I love to play songs for each other. We hear them and explain why they remind us of the other. I want us to just curl up at the end of the day, appreciating each other and how damn lucky we are, while we listen to a nice story about a murder in a small town. We won't even need a sitter. We'll fall asleep so fast anyway.

I DISAPPEAR SO HARD

When you're pregnant, you can't go to the post office without a well-meaning busybody dropping parenting knowledge on you. "It goes by so fast." "Sleep while the baby sleeps." "Wine equals liquid patience." Actually, that last one is helpful. But you know what no one tells you before you become a parent, you guys? No one tells you that you are going to perform an amaaaaaazing magic trick. You are going to . . . disappear.

It happens almost instantly. One day, you are shaking your hair and getting a lot of "This one's on me," and the next, poof, you're gone. It sucks. If you're a hot twenty-something carrying a phone and a key fob outside an apartment building, you will have the door opened for you, but if you're a lady pushing a double stroller and a toddler fussing under one arm? Forget it. Sure, people might look right through you. Heck, they might even talk as though you're not there. But ignore us at your own peril, because when the shit hits the fan—*Abracadabra!*—moms are the only ones with a Tide stick.

JEN

Your eyes work so differently after you become a mom. How you see the world, other children, and other moms changes. I guess maybe your hearing works differently too, because you start to notice people saying things like "This is not your mom's Toyota" and "These aren't your mom's jeans." Like it's a *big* insult for something to be a "mom's [whatever]." You are saying that the thing is lame. Really? The Dude from *The Big Lebowski* wears a housecoat around, isn't too on top of his personal maintenance, and isn't even making sure miniature humans can name their shapes, but he gets admiringly called "The Dude" and we get called lame? Well, I call bullshit.

I don't think I need to tell other moms how important moms are. We are Atlas. We hold up the earth while everyone else is putting stickers all over it. Since the dawn of time, women have been having the babies, taking care of the babies, and making the babies into humans that others can stand to be around, and most of the time, no one notices. Nobody sees the time and effort (and heartache) that goes into being a mom. Except for other moms.

I remember seeing a friend at a party when her baby was about two months old. It was her first time out without a sitter, but it seemed like she was doing pretty well. I pulled her aside and said, "I'm so impressed with you! You look great, and the fact that you're even out of the house with such a young one is amazing! I couldn't have a conversation with anyone until the baby was about four months. I didn't even know my name. You're killin' it!" She gave me a nod like, *Okay, whatever*, and I assumed, yet again, that I was the weirdo.

About six months later, she sent me an email. She thanked me for saying that to her, because she felt so out of it, so unable to have an adult conversation, so removed from the outside world, and she thought it was just her. Oh, girl. I see you. I *am* you. And not everyone who does notice you will see you in the right way anymore. I'm still flirty, sexy, and smart and know how to shotgun a beer, but I just don't have time to make sure you notice it.

As we've gotten more attention for our videos, we've had a few companies approach us to ask if we would work with them— you know, like how Sprite asked LeBron, only we're shorter, whiter, and will do things for paychecks with about six fewer zeros. We don't say yes all that often because we're very particular— we're not planning to whore out our IMOMSOHARD moms for just anyone, but we know you guys will understand when we agree to talk about something we like on our videos for some babysitter money.

So yeah, every once in a while we say yes to a collaboration. A few months ago, we were doing a promotion with a company, and we showed up to the fitting. We were so psyched. I mean, a "fitting"—who are we, Gisele? The rep greeted us, showed us the massive cheese plate we'd requested, and went over the details of the shoot for us. The idea was that we were just a couple of moms at a coffee shop. Got it. It was going to be a stretch, but we were feeling good about our ability to get into character and pull it off. A tall, pretty stylist came over and led us to Wardrobe. We each ducked into our little changing areas and put on what they'd chosen for us to wear. Cue fun movie montage of us laughing and trying on adorable outfits.

Except not at all. When I saw the clothes they had chosen for us, my mood went flat fast. A moment that should have been incredible just felt . . . bad. We didn't expect them to hit it so hard on the head on the first shot that we'd say, "Girl, that is it. Don't even try anything else on." But the outfit they put Kristin in was like they went to the store where Amish ladies buy their clothes, looked around, and then said, "Do you have anything that isn't quite so sexy?"

Kristin came out of her changing area with her head down, and I thought, *Absolutely not. Neither one of us would wear that to clean the garage. If you gave me that outfit for free at Kohl's, I wouldn't take it home with me.* They'd put her in a sad cardigan, a shapeless knit top, elastic-waist pants, and orthopedic shoes. Now, I know Kristin will proudly rock some baggy shorts and a pair of Tevas, but these clothes were not channeling her fun camp counselor vibe. They were just terribly fitting, insulting clothes. We weren't headed to Bingo Night. You want to upset me to my core? Suggest that I might wear khaki capris. I will punch your face.

I turned to the stylist and said, "She would never wear that. I would never wear that. Is this what you would buy?" Kristin was like, "Yeah, we kind of dress like you, only in a bigger size because we've had a couple kids."

It pissed me off, you know? Listen, I know that I am not twenty-two anymore—I still have a Hotmail account. I look at younger women and I get it, really, I do. Who wouldn't want to either be or touch someone that radiates life with the intensity of a thousand suns? But hey, sweet young things, you might scream "I'm fertile" with every sculpted curve and smooth, flat tummy, but you know what else screams fertility? Two kids. I'm not asexual. I'm just tired. It's demoralizing that when you cross the line into being a mom, some people define you by that and that alone, not your unstoppable karaoke skills, your deep interest in nineteenth-century poetry, or the way you run a meeting so everyone's out of there in ten minutes flat.

The crazy thing was, when we came in, Kristin had been wearing almost exactly what the stylist was wearing, except it wasn't as tight. She was rocking a concert tee, denim, and black high tops. She looked hot. And normal. Not like she had just stepped out of the St. John's Bay catalog or an ad for arthritis medication.

Somewhere along the line, moms have been told, "Sorry! You're not a perfect size 0, so it doesn't matter what you wear. You're done. You're just going to wear something that covers you up so we don't have to look at you. Is there a drop cloth around here?" If you buy into that line of thinking, it's over. You might as well disappear.

Here's the thing, Asshole Who Gave the Wardrobe Department Directions for This Shoot: you know that woman you married, who you found exotic and mysterious and alluring because she liked listening to avant-garde music and dressed cool? She didn't change because you knocked her up. Your seed is powerful, but not that powerful, sir. It's not unicorn glitter. She didn't turn into your grandma because she got a little of it on her (that sounded gross, but you know what I mean). She was awesome before. She's still got all those interests; she's still badass. *And* she made a baby. She might have a different focus right now and for the next few years. She'll get back to that other stuff later—or not. But nobody puts Baby in a corner, and nobody puts this mom in a denim shirt with *Looney Tunes* embroidered on it.

Don't say I'm "just a mom," and don't make me look like I hate my life. I want to feel good and high-five another woman because our lives are awesome. I wake up in the morning in a house with three people who love me to the moon and back. I have friends who I would swallow a fistful of thumbtacks for (though I cannot imagine a scenario where that would be required), and I make moms laugh for a living. I love my life.

I'm proud as hell that we got them to change the clothes on that shoot. We gave them a stern talking to and sent them to bed without dinner. Not really, but we did put our foot down. We gave them the option of dressing and presenting us how we wanted, or we'd walk. 'Cause I know it's not just me out there, you guys. I'm you and all your mom friends too. No one likes to be underestimated, and you better believe I know how lucky I am to have this chance to show the world what moms are about, and I'll be damned if I will let them put us in a box. Or khaki capris.

KRISTIN

I'd love to say it's just the ad execs of the world who are guilty of writing us off into the land of baggy beige pants, but sometimes even other moms can be guilty of it too.

During a Facebook Live event we did a few months ago, I wore one of my favorite pairs of jeans, which happen to be ripped. We take pride in our comment section because the moms are just cool. They're laid-back and positive. But one woman, who was probably having a crappy day, wrote in to say, "Oh, honey, don't you think those jeans are a little young . . ." She knee-shamed me! Let's be clear, folks, I wasn't wearing bootie shorts and a tube top (man, I wish I could). There was *one* rip in the knee, and I paid like an extra $50 for that rip. I had paired the jeans with a really cute Anthropologie jacket with flowers all over it, but it was too much for this lady. And let me tell ya something, I ain't giving up without a fight. Until my last breath, I will be wearing stuff like that. What *I* like. Not what you think I should like. I know you'd rather I disappeared into age-appropriate, knee-having mom jeans, but that would be prioritizing my role as a mom over my role as, well, me. The only thing about my body that is a ten is my jean size. I like wearing clothes that are a little rock 'n' roll, and on my deathbed I will be wearing a leather motorcycle jacket and sweet tennis shoes. If I waited until I was "perfect" to enjoy some of the clothes I like, I'd be wearing a muumuu until I flatlined.

These days, I like a good jean, a great tee, and a strong lip.

Jen loves to wear makeup. I know for a fact that she uses a product that lists cloned human foreskin cells as one of the ingredients. Twice a day. I'm not saying it doesn't pay off. Someday, she'll be eighty-two and everyone will swear she's eighty. I, on the other hand, tend to stay out of beauty stores. I can't take the carnival barkers: "You with the big pores, step right up" or "You there, that's right, you with the dark circles, test your luck with our Totally Ineffective—But Don't Worry, Also Criminally Expensive—Lotions and Potions."

I'll be the first to admit that I've never been very good about buying beauty supplies. I can buy all of my makeup at CVS, and I have two lipsticks—that I stole from Jen. But that's not something to brag about. I hit a low point when someone gave me three $100 gift cards to Bath & Body Works one year. Everything there is already like five for $30, so just how bad did they think I smelled? Maybe it's because my beauty routine involves splashing the kids' dirty-butt bathwater on my face to get the topsoil off. Which is to say my makeup bag is about the size of a Ziploc snack bag and used to contain primarily a wide selection of regular and medicated ChapSticks.

But when we started doing videos, Jen looked at me and said, "You know, you look really pretty with lipstick." I was like, "Okay, great. Thanks." She said, real slow and deliberate, "No. You look really pretty with lipstick." And I said, "Wait, are you telling me I have to wear lipstick?" She replied, "No. I'm not telling you that you have to. I'm telling you that you look really pretty when you wear it." And I was like, "I look really pretty in lipstick." She just Jedi-ed me.

Jen offered to let me borrow some of her lipstick to try it out. I went into her bathroom, and her vanity has got tons of drawers; it's like a MAC counter in there. Jen has a Caboodle that's about the size of a bar cart. There were so, so many colors of lipstick to choose from. I picked a saucy red shade, and I put it on. Later, when I noticed myself on videos, I thought, *Wow, I do a lip, and it* does *make my eyes look better, and I do look happier. And it's pretty. I feel pretty. Huh.*

I started to wear more lipstick and care a little bit. At first, it was just because I was on camera, and then I decided, *All right. Let's do this.* It makes me happy. And Jen makes me feel like a million bucks when I wear it. She'll say, "The second you put on lipstick, your eyes pop." My husband says the same thing.

Now, putting on lipstick has become a teeny tiny act of everyday defiance. It doesn't matter what you weigh, it doesn't matter what size you are, it doesn't matter what you're wearing—you can put on lipstick. Wearing lipstick means I'm paying attention to me, just this much. I'm still sexual, and I'm still beautiful. I might be dead emotionally and physically—I might be tired AF—but I'm still a woman. It's like armor that comes in Crimson Ice and Breathing Fire. Bad. Ass.

Let's say I have a full-on mom day where I am just all manage and hustle from morning to night. If I have a lipstick in my cup holder, and I put that on my lips, I go into whatever it is I'm going to do with a little more swagger. I'm going to push a stroller, I'm going to have barf in my hair, I'm going to smell like poop, my thighs are going to rub together, but I'm going to have a strong freaking lip. You may not know my name, but you are going to know my thunder.

It's literally your mouthpiece. Literally. Read my lips: Your voice matters. When I put on a fresh coat, I'm saying, "This person has ideas. This person has things to say," and they're coming out. This isn't a scared person. When you go to drop your kid off, you might have some color on your teeth or have lipstick streaked across your face or in your hair, but if you wear some fire engine red lipstick and get in a fight in the carpool lane, it's a whole other ballgame.

So you know what? Go buy a Chanel lipstick for $40. Or go buy yourself something at the CVS. I'm wearing tinted Burt's Bees right now (what can I say, my lips are dry a lot). It costs $8 for a four pack. It doesn't matter. Every time you put it on, you will feel like a warrior.

If lipstick isn't your thing, find something else, just one little thing for you, because I guarantee you have done five hundred things for everyone else in your life before breakfast. We all have that thing that reminds us who we are at the core.

After I had Eleanor, I was really heavy for a long time. Unlike every nursing mother I knew who lost weight when she nursed (except Jen), I gained weight and kept it on. It wasn't reasonable weight. My shoulders were fat, my neck was fat, my ass was wide, and my boobs looked like sideways watermelons. I would look in the mirror and just sob. I didn't know how to dress this body. I wore maternity pants for a year after the baby. I wouldn't buy myself anything because I wanted to wait until I was me again. I wore my husband's T-shirts, old tattered leggings, or "fat pants" with oversize button-ups. It was like I had completely lost myself. Finally, I stopped nursing, and my weight dropped. I was a size 10. I am still a size 10. I weigh fifteen pounds more now than I did when I got pregnant with Eleanor. All I did was try and try to get back to the old me, so much so that I tore my shoulder and my hip during one very unreasonable CrossFit class (Groupon). And then one day, I said to myself, *What if this is it? What if this is your new normal?* And I went to Nordstrom Rack and bought myself new clothes. Do I look in the mirror every day and say, "Wow, you look amazing!"? No. But I look in the mirror and I say, "I recognize this chick and I like her."

The messed up thing about disappearing in other people's eyes is that you can start to diminish how you see yourself too. How we spend our time says a lot about who we are. And if we're spending all of our time doing 80 billion things for other people all day long, no wonder they see us just as snot wiper, sock finder, lunch maker, and yeller atter instead of as a person on our own. Part of getting seen, of being recognized as a person in the world, is setting aside some time for yourself. Maybe it's a hip-hop dance class once a week. Maybe it's going to a concert. Maybe it's treating yourself to the perfect pair of ankle boots. Maybe it's planning a girls-only camping trip. That stuff matters. It sends a signal: *Hey, I'm here. I might empty your puke bucket when you're sick, but I can also set up a tent in ten minutes like a pro.* I think our kids notice it when we set aside time for ourselves too.

When she grows up and goes to college, I want Eleanor to say to herself, *You know what? I have great grades, I work hard, and I have a part-time job at a bagel shop. I'm going to spend $100 on myself at LifeSpa.* I would be like, "My job here is done."

You do not have to pay a mint to go to a fancy spa day (but if you can, do you, girl). You can Groupon that business. I go to the drugstore and get these little booties that I wear sometimes that moisturize my feet because I have rough heels. If you've saved for your family by couponing and going to Bed Bath & Beyond with your 20 percent off, you've earned the right to take a second for yourself. I'm not always very good at it myself, but I try.

Personally, I've only had four or five facials in my life. One time, I was having a facial and the way she was touching my face was so tender that for the first ten minutes I felt uncomfortable. Then I realized, *Oh, it's because she's being so nice to me and I'm calm.* I started to cry a little bit, and then a little bit more until I was sobbing. She said, "You're okay, honey." She totally knew what she was going on. "This is not uncommon. You're just relaxing, probably for the first time in months."

Yes, I thought, *I shouldn't relax just right now. This is something I should do regularly.* So I learned to relax a little more because I deserve it.

Self-care is really hard as a mother. Somewhere along the way, there was some shitty Hallmark card that told us if we give all of our time to our kids and husbands they will be better people. It's so untrue. Mothers who sacrifice everything gain nothing. Before we were mothers, we were women. And we still are. We gain nothing by missing a gyno appointment to make it to our kid's volleyball game. We gain nothing by skipping our wine night with the girls to organize the garage. And we gain nothing by struggling in darkness without a few rays of light. We work this hard out of love, but we gotta shine the love light on ourselves once in a while. It makes us better people. It makes us happier moms. It makes us healthier women.

Just tell your husband, "I need two hours in the bathroom by myself." Get some trashy magazines, get yourself some cucumber water, get yourself a scrub, and just do all this stuff for no reason other than it's for you. That's not selfish, that's karma. It's not always a bitch. Sometimes, it's a soak in some lavender bath salts, and girl, you damn well deserve it.

I LOVE ON SOME LADIES SO HARD

Imagine bringing a visitor from another planet to Earth and telling her, "Yeah, so, these people over here with the curves and stuff, they keep track of all the schedules, make all the food that keeps everyone alive, put sunscreen on folks so they don't get incinerated by the sun, and—oh, yeah— create other humans inside their midsections. And then you have these people over here who can't converse while they microwave something—but they can lift stuff. Guess who's in charge?" The alien would be like, "Nu-uhhhhhhhh!"

We hear you, alien sister. Women are *so freaking awesome*. And we love all of y'all. In fact, sometimes we *love* you love you. Yeah, we're talking about how every once in a while you meet a gal who is just a Beyoncé-level lady—with the good hair, the right amount of bounce, and the ability to crack a wicked joke—and that appreciation ratchets up the intensity. You get all nervous and awkward around her, and you develop a good old-fashioned girl crush. (Calm down, fellas. A girl crush isn't always about girl-on-girl action, so get your minds out of Pornhub mode. This is us celebrating women, because heroes can have boobs too.)

The two of us can girl-crush with the best of 'em. When we were younger, we both had a thing for Daisy Duke. Who wouldn't, right? Those legs that never stopped, that cool hair, her hoop earrings, that sweet little accent when she was talking to Boss Hogg? Girlfriend wore heels all the time and she lived *on a farm*. What?!

These days, we get a little weak-kneed for a brassy dame who has her act together, the kind of gal who knows how to roll with the punches and doesn't pull any. We feel such intense love for women. It's one of the best things about when we tour: we get to see so many of you, and damn if it's not inspiring.

When we look out in the crowd, we know that moms are there to see us and be around their friends. Moms get dressed up, grab some appetizers and cocktails, and lose their minds when they see one another. They're so excited about new haircuts and new clothes. We feel like we're phantoms next to those women in the audience because we can feel their delight. We want to look out at the crowd and just say, "We see you." We see you trying, we see you looking fly, and we love it. There is nothing like a mob of moms celebrating our collective boss power to restore your faith in the universe.

KRISTIN

My current girl crush (besides Jen—she's typing this) is this gal we work with; her name is Nickole. I want to be friends with her so bad. She is one of those women who is so beautiful it makes me a little angry, and when I encounter one of these women, I can't stop watching her mouth, so you know she thinks I am a total creep. She moves like a panther: half sexy slink, half top-of-the-food-chain-and-I-know-it swagger. I tried to walk like that, but when you're wearing a Spanx tank and jeans with ketchup stains, you just look like an extra from *Breaking Bad*. Anytime she's around, I start to act dorky and say weird stuff like "I love Pilates too!," which is bullshit, 'cause I do not *at all* love Pilates. When I see her, I think, *I really like her. Or do I* like *her?* I can't tell if I want to Single White Female her life or have a light make-out sesh. Like, do I want to kiss her or wear her skin as a suit? (Note to HR: I joke, I joke! Her skin would never fit me, she's like a size 2.)

I love a good girl crush. It just feels good all over to see another woman out there killing it. When I hear about the "mommy wars" and how women get in cat fights with one another, I'm like, *Where are you hanging out, man? The green room for Maury Povich?* Sure, maybe not every woman out there is crushing it in the empathy department day in and day out—every gal has her day when she could use a "W" in an unintentional "Who Wore It Best?" showdown—but for the most part, what we see when we're out on the road is that women are *awesome* to one another. And moms especially. While we're on tour, we peek through our dressing room windows and watch the moms walk into the venues. There are thousands of women throwing their heads back in laughter and strutting around in killer shoes. When we were in Houston, our tour bus was parked in front of the theater, and three women climbed a tree, trying to see inside. They were laughing so hard it looked like the tree was going to break in half, but they were having so much fun, just going for it.

We can't even count the number of letters, cards, bottles of wine, sweatshirts, T-shirts, chocolates, cookies, lotions, and oils—and the occasional vagina spray—that moms send to us in our dressing room. Jen and I cheer like we won the lottery *every single time*. Women are awesome in general: awesome to their kids, awesome to their husbands, and awesome to one another. Our shows are like monster truck rallies for moms, and I tell ya, that vibe is a shot of Fireball to the soul.

I have so many current crushes I can't keep them straight: Lady Gaga, Allison Janney, Jennifer Garner, Mindy Kaling, Tiffany Haddish, Jenna Bush, Amy Poehler, Tina Fey, Melissa McCarthy, Sandra Bullock, Cate Blanchett, Kristen Wiig, Michelle Obama, Kathryn Hahn, anyone who was on the TV show *Friends*—the list is endless. While regular crushes are pretty superficial, I think there is a deeper appreciation at the heart of a true-blue girl crush: like the one I have on my sister, who lives her single life loud and strong; my friend Laura, who is a writer and occupational therapist; my friend Jenny Tesler, who has a daughter with Rett syndrome and fund-raises like a gangster to help find a cure; and my friends Lynn and Danelle, who raise their kids in Nebraska like mom bosses. And my friend Ally, who stepped up as a stepmom. We see all of the stuff in our friends that other people might not notice—how hard they worked to get dinner on the table after knocking 'em dead all day at work, how they were there when we needed someone to say, "Damn, that sounds hard," and how they knew that effortless style actually takes a boatload of effort. That feeling of being seen and understood by another person is incredible, which is why my female friendships are so essential to my mental stability. That's what's so great about womanhood. We can just appreciate the hell out of one another.

Jen is excellent at complimenting women. She'll run into a woman she doesn't even know who's all blinged out, and she'll squeal with delight, "Oh, my gosh! You look fantastic! Check out your necklace! I love it so much!" And women light up like a fire: "Omigosh, I just got it today. Thank you so much!" Jen says all the right things. It's an explosion of girl enthusiasm. It's so high-pitched that wineglasses shatter and dogs begin to howl. If they've got cleavage, Jen gestures to the boob zone with her small doll hands. "Look at those boobs!" She knows women love it. Also, she just likes to talk about boobs. This is where I'm out of my element because my approach is more that of an aggressive hugger. Then I tank and ask weird questions like "Did you put your snow tires on yet?" or "What was the interest rate on your home loan? I think you should consider refinancing." Very sexy. However, I am a good hugger.

Jen says that sometimes I compliment with a fair amount of anger. I do this for sure. I'll shout, "Jen! Stop saying you don't look good! Those pants are amazing, and your butt looks fantastic!" Most of the time, I compliment like a coach: "You're doing great. When you get back in there, I want you to focus on keeping your butt low when you're lifting that kid. Don't let him overwork you."

I gotta get better at this. I have to learn to say things like "Hey, you've got a nice haircut."

I also want to teach Eleanor how to celebrate other women. Hmm. We've got some ground to cover there. Before the end of school last year, I read a story for her class, and she got to sit next to me. Every kid in there was so excited. I'm not gonna lie, I gave a great performance. I knew my demo. I got in there, I read the story (*Gerald the Giraffe*), I did the voices, I hit the right notes. It brought the house down, and when I was done, I looked over at Eleanor and she just looked sad.

I asked, "What's the matter?" She said, "You did not let me look at those pictures enough when you were showing them." Tough crowd.

It was pretty deflating. I mean, girl, I gave that my *all*, so I said, "You know what, Eleanor? That hurts my feelings. You should focus on what I did well and not what I could do better. You gotta support your girls even when your 'girl' is your mama. What you should be saying is, 'Good job, Mommy.'" I just want to teach her that it's important to support another person doing her thing, especially if they kill as hard as I did.

Then she said, "It was kind of good." Listen, I'll take it. But next time, I want a high five and a compliment on my English accent.

There are definitely a few women who make me feel a little something you-know-where in my don't-know-why. For the longest time it was Angelina Jolie. She'd be into me, right? She's such a badass, but, like, a real compassionate badass who wants to do her part for third-world countries. We have the same bone structure, and we both love camping. (Angie, *call me*.)

And we're back to the essence of what draws us to a woman we get a crush on. It's not just that we see something in another woman that we lack. It's that we see something in another woman that reminds us of what's amazing about ourselves. There is a deep level of "I get you, girl, and I have a feeling you'd get me too."

Besides, let's be honest, even if I did manage to get up close and personal with Angelina Jolie, I wouldn't know what to do with her lady parts. I shouldn't be giving directions to anyone about how to navigate my own private area let alone handling someone else's. I didn't even know we had three holes down there until I had a baby. It would be so awkward; I'd end up in a belly button, saying, "Do you like that? Does this feel good?"

I would cuddle, though. Maybe hold a hand or something. And I'm pretty sure I would *love* being married to a woman because she would understand what "Can you turn the TV up a tad?" means. Instead of angrily handing me the remote and saying, "Here, you do it," she would understand that one click up or down makes a difference. My husband will turn it up sixteen clicks, and then when I say, "Hey, maybe a little less?" he just goes, "Uggggggggh," like I am some impossible-to-please volume nazi. I just like to turn it down when it's the scary stuff so our kids don't hear it, but you'd think I was asking him for a third child. It's like for him there are two volumes: off and LOUD. Hey, man, can we just meet in the middle somewhere and see where that gets us?

TV was where I saw all of my favorite girls as a kid: Dolly Parton, Carol Burnett, and the entire cast of *The Golden Girls*.

179

(These shows were all in syndication, by the way, so don't go doing the math on my age.) Those ladies would *get me*. I've seen every episode of *The Golden Girls* about eighty-nine times. Dorothy, Sophia, Blanche, and Rose? I'm a mix of all of 'em. I love how they were out there, dating and humping in their sixties. Yes, their husbands were dead or whatever, but that didn't even really matter because the important part was that they had one another. The men were totally incidental. The heart of the show was how they were always there for one another, which seemed like a dream. I mean, wouldn't you love to live with your besties in a house in Florida after your husband kicks it? We could all just share the laughter and love and a nice cheesecake—and then I'd thank you for being a friend.

JEN

You guys, that show was genius, but it made me sad. I was so scared Sophia was going to die all the time. I can't do sad shows. I'd rather do a spin class than watch *Old Yeller*. I'm a crier, and I don't recover easily. However, I'd probably watch *The Golden Girls* with Kristin. Being married to Kristin would be a dream. Easy. We'd watch TV together and I'd say, "How's the volume? Is this good? Let's have a bottle of chardonnay and then talk about *Serial* and *Making a Murderer*." We'd go out to dinner anytime we didn't feel like cooking, and we could split an appetizer without a fuss. You ask a man if he wants to split something with you, and he'll say, "That's all I'm going to have for the rest of the night??? Does this mean no treats at the movie?" Women will be like, "Let's split the lettuce wraps, a salad, and a side of fries, and we'll get a dessert if we still need it."

I've had my fair share of girl crushes. For me, it's never really "Can I get some of that?" It's more like "Can I get that? Like, can I have some genetic modifications to make me a little more like that?"

I have super weird taste in women. I was into the Boone Sisters. Oh, you don't know who they are? Perhaps you are not fifty-eight years old. (To be clear, neither am I, friends. I just know how to spread the love around.) Debby Boone sang "You Light Up My Life," my favorite song from ages zero to ten. I used to sit by my window, just as she suggested in the song, and dream about Bo Duke, wondering why he didn't love me. My dad told me I had about fifteen years before marrying John Schneider was even an option on the table. Thank God for unanswered prayers, amiright? But those Boone Sisters with their perfectly feathered hair and puffed sleeves . . . they were my kind of women.

On the more traditional side, I also liked Sloane from *Ferris Bueller's Day Off*, Mercedes from *License to Drive*, Patricia Arquette, Courteney Cox, Helen Hunt, and SJP and the entire cast of *SATC*. I had a crush on Blair from *Facts of Life*, and Jo too. I couldn't decide. Then there's Tootie—she's real hot now, and she doesn't take crap from anyone. #squadgoals. Lisa Bonet is amazing. She is so poetic, so pretty, and she has that sexy, feathery voice. And she's married to Khal Drogo.

But for me, it's tough to beat Michelle Pfeiffer from *Grease 2*. She's got the jawline and those crystal eyeballs and mad femme fatale energy. Girlfriend was *Catwoman*. Michelle Pfeiffer today at sixty-whatever is hotter than I have been any day of my life. All I can say is, she'd better not be funny or good at math, otherwise I am going to *have words* with whoever doles out the luck.

But do you who know my weirdest girl crush was? My grandma. She was so enigmatic and cool, her makeup was on point, and she slept late. She was a beautician, and she had a sweet dressing room in her house that had a huge round mirror with light bulbs around it and an elegant little wire chair. There was a drawer in her dressing table that had nothing but different perfumes, and the whole top of the table was lined with tubes of every color lipstick and nail polish and eyeshadow imaginable. If she was going to the grocery store, she did all of it. She did her face. She did her big hair. Big lashes. Big everything. I used to love sitting next to her and looking up at her, talking to her and watching her make herself ready for the world. I learned so much about being a woman from her, about taking the time to treat myself right, and now, when I get myself ready for my day, I channel a little of that grandma energy. I am going to make the best old lady. I already own some seriously chunky jewelry, and it just keeps getting bigger as time goes by.

Like I said, I'm not saying I want to hump anyone (see Grandma, above), but there are a couple of women I would maybe take a bath with. Mostly, it's musicians. I always think musicians are talking directly to me when they're singing. I have a crush on Kelly Clarkson. I really loved Tiffany when I was a kid (I might not be fifty-eight, but I am old enough to have listened to Tiffany on my Sony Walkman), and I would most certainly take a bath with Stevie Nicks. I've had a pretty significant girl crush on Stevie Nicks for a loooooong time. She's so chill and rock-starry at the same time, and she wears big velvety clothes and cool hats. I'm a fan on her Facebook page. I had all of her albums growing up. I just feel like we should hang out. She lives not far from me—or so I've heard. Not that I've googled her or asked everyone I met if they know her or at least where she lives. I saw her live on October 3, 2003. I didn't cut my hair for ten years after that so I could look more like her. So far exactly zero people have mistaken me for Stevie Nicks. Perhaps it's time for me to invest more heavily in hats and shawls.

The other thing I really love about Stevie is her combination of vulnerability and strength. I'd love if I could transfer some of that to Delilah. I worry sometimes that I'm not hitting the right balance of girliness and toughness for her. I don't want to send her the message that it's not okay to be girlie—'cause I hate that "girlie" has become like a dirty word to some people. If my girl wants sequins and glitter pens, if those make her feel powerful, screw you if you want to give her—or me—a hard time about it. But I also want to make sure she can take what the world hands her.

Kristin and I both have older boys and younger girls, and I catch myself—and other people—treating them differently occasionally. Someone will tell our boys to "toughen up" when things don't go their way, but they'd never say that to Delilah, so I have a confession: when Dash is pestering her and she straight-up clotheslines him, I will very loudly say, "We do not lay our hands on other people," but then I will quietly pull her aside and fist-bump her because I am proud that she stood up for herself. I want her to be strong, not scared. I want her to be the kind of girl that other girls get girl crushes on because she is such a boss.

In the end, here's how I feel about girl crushes: they are totally normal. There has never been one moment of my life when I thought, *Should I not be looking at Daisy Duke that way?* I just love a lot of people, *especially* women. Women have fewer harsh edges than men. We let more people in emotionally, and we have that gift that allows us to love pretty much anyone. I'm sure it's ovary-related. And I think a lot of women are this way, because women are welcoming. Dudes think women are catty, but I think women are cool and supportive. I bet men picture us aggressively pillow-fighting—topless—over which one of us gets to serve them beer, but that ain't the case. Sure, I might covet someone's itty-bitty waist and round thing in your face, but that doesn't mean that I wouldn't love to invite that curvy broad over to binge on cheesecake and *CSI*. I like to compliment something specific about a woman—her hairstyle, her legs, her boobs—even if it seems like she doesn't need the boost. Guess what? She does. We all do. I want to work up the nerve to just walk up to a woman and tell her that I think she's amazing. I think we should all start doing just that—become like a secret network of moms boosting each other, loving on each other, and lifting each other up. Let the revolution begin.

IT TAKES A VILLAGE SO HARD

We don't want to be cavewomen—too much fire tending and water gathering, not enough binge watching and living past thirty—but there is something alluring about the tribe mentality. We dig the idea that if your little monkey is breaking away from the pack, someone else will grab him by the wrist and bring him back into the herd as if he were her own child.

In our neighborhoods growing up, we knew we couldn't get away with jack because even if our moms weren't around to call us on something stupid we were about to do, Mrs. Mitchell or Mr. Adams would be up on our butt so fast we wouldn't even have time to crack open our Orange Crush and Pop Rocks.

Beyond the care and feeding and the picking of nits, we're responsible for shaping future adults so that they don't turn into little a-holes. Our feeling is that when your kid steps out of line, there should be an attitude of "I know what I'd want someone to say to my kid if she did that," followed by a carefully chosen sharp word. We'll all be better for it in the long run. Let's assume we all want the same thing: to raise decent human beings who will be protected from danger until they are old enough to file their own taxes.

JEN

*While Kristin and I are kind of do-your-thing, we-love-*you-the-way-you-are, proud-to-be-you-and-me types, we're still mama bears at heart, and when something or someone hurts our kids, it's a game changer. You're with me here, right? Your kid is threatened, and all of a sudden you're putting down your purse, you're taking off your earrings, and you're saying, "I'm going to fight a four-year-old right now. This one I won't lose."

You punch my kid, you deal with the big, blond bouncer with him—that's me. My Nebraska mom comes out. I don't suffer meanness on the playground. I'll yell at anybody's kids, and I mean I'll *yell*. If my kid's playing with the group and it's getting a little physical or something, my inner military brat kicks in, and I'll announce, "Alright, everybody, the rule is everybody shares. Come at me, bro, if you've got a problem with sharing at the park." Kids are little id-driven heathens bent on satisfying their own selfish urges. We've all got to pitch in and take responsibility for managing the pack.

Do you know what I tell my kids to do if we get separated? "Find a mommy." They're easy to identify, and I know they'll help. They will return my kid to me with the same urgency as I would return theirs to them. And then we will both cry and wish we could have a drink.

I think most moms are pretty good about stepping in to make things right when needed, but there was one time—and this is the only time that anything like this had happened, so I remember it really well—where a mom let me down hard. I had brought my two-year-old son to a mall play area, which is a mecca for moms and a petri dish for hand, foot and mouth disease. You just know you're going to walk out with someone else's stuff and some sort of infection when you sign the release. I have never come home from one of those places without the kids having some kind of barf situation over the next few days. Anyway, on a day when the promise of ten minutes where I was not solely responsible for providing entertainment for my toddler outweighed the risk of an outbreak, we went to this play area near our house. All the moms, all the nannies, they're all in the same boat. They fill out the forms and are like, "Now go play and give me two seconds so I can catch up on a little email exchange and some texts."

I lost my son for just *a second* behind this giant hot dog statue, and then I heard him scream. I ran over, and his arm was in this other kid's mouth, and I shouted, "No, no, no, no, no, no, no, no, no!" I got his arm out of the kid's mouth, and then the kid slapped him in the face. I stood up, shocked. I caught another mom's eye, and she said, "That's not the first time that's happened today." I just freaked out. I pointed at the kid and yelled, "Whose kid is this?" I screamed it over the whole food court. "Show yourself!" Here's the crazy thing: she did

187

not. There was no parent around. That's why this really stuck with me. For the most part, every mom would be horrified and would give you a long monologue: "We're going through a biting phase. I don't know where it came from. My child is not an animal. My husband and I don't bite. No one in our family bites. I don't know why this is happening. I'm so sorry. Can I drive him to urgent care for you?" On and on until you finally offered to buy her a latte to calm her down and show there's no hard feelings. You get it. It's a nonstop project, getting your kid to show respect, kindness, and a proper understanding of what goes in your mouth and what is another human being.

The mom was probably having a rough day and had her headphones on listening to Adele somewhere, trying to remember what it was like to be called by her given name instead of "Peyton's mom." God bless her. I know we can't be vigilant every moment of every day (I mean, I lost my kid behind a novelty-size frankfurter), but I think everything would be better if everyone took the attitude that we're all pitching in all the time. Just look out for one another.

I used to get so mad when I had a newborn in the stroller and tried to go in somewhere to get coffee, and someone would let the door fall on me, you know? Or they would get irritated and act like it was such a huge fricking inconvenience when they had to get out of the way of the stroller. One day, when I'd had it, I said to this guy rolling his eyes as I struggled to push a stroller up some stairs, "It's sort of like a wheelchair, okay? He can't walk; he's four months old. Is that what you do to somebody in a wheelchair who can't walk? You get all huffy about it? WTF?"

It's so weird that people have no compassion for moms, so moms have to have compassion for moms. Kristin's really good at it. When she sees someone having a hard time, she'll just take over. She won't even ask sometimes. She just starts doing.

We'll be in mid-conversation when suddenly she'll hand me her (tiny) bag and say, "Hold on one second." Next thing I know, Kristin will be next to a mom who's trying to juggle an iced tea, a three-year-old with poop face, and an infant, saying, "Excuse me. Yeah, hi. Do you want me to hold the baby while you do that?" And then Kristin's got the baby and we pick our conversation back up. "And anyway, I found a 20 percent off coupon . . . Can I have his binkie? And then . . . Mom, do you need to go potty? Well, do that and come back. We got this." People sometimes start to say no, but I tell them it goes faster if they just give in and let her put the Splenda in their coffee for them.

I love that stuff. It's the kind of thing you know happens in the Midwest, where families are looking out for people's kids when they're running in a pack through backyards. I always thought my mom was part of some mom mafia. She somehow always heard what we were up to, even if we left the house early that morning and hadn't come back until dinner or streetlights turned on. She knew that I'd eaten a bologna sandwich at the Bortels' house or that I left my bike in the Rowlands' driveway. I thought it was deep-level spy stuff, but it was really just moms calling one another: "Your kid is here. Used our bathroom. Ate a Popsicle. Said the word 'damn.' Let me know if you see my kid."

Now that we live in California, I get less of that hometown village feeling, but every once in a while, I get a flash of it and it fills my bucket, as the teachers say these days. Like when I got my nails done for the first time after Dash was born. I brought him into the salon I love. He was so, so tiny. I brought everything I could think of to keep him happy—white noise machine, blanket, mobile that attached to the stroller—and the women who worked there shook their heads at me and all the stuff I had brought to distract him. They took him out of the stroller and passed him around. They didn't even ask. They just loved on my baby. I know we're all buried in our phones and disconnected so much of the time, but those moments of connection—that's what I want in life.

KRISTIN

We had the same thing happen with Eleanor in a restaurant! There was this great little Persian place close to where we used to live. We would take her in there, and the woman who was working front of house would stop working to go hold Eleanor, and she'd say, "Look at this baby. Look at these eyes." It was like her new job was introducing Eleanor to all of the customers, not finding them a table and making Tah Dig.

We get wrapped up in being polite, and we get reluctant to reach out to other people in a friendly way. I think it's because we sort of feel like we're coming off as creepy. Or when we see someone who could use a hand, we think, *Oh, I don't want to offend her and make her feel like she doesn't have it together.* But you just know if she were on the other side of it—if she were the one watching you struggle—she'd be more than willing to help if you needed it. I just believe in giving everyone a break—and the benefit of the doubt.

Like Jen, the only time I get a little critical toward another parent is maybe if there's a lack of discipline when there's a group of families playing together. If my kid is being naughty on the playground, I absolutely want you to put him in check if his behavior could be hurting someone else. I promise, my kids are not angels, and you better expect that I'm going to do the same because neither are yours. If your kid is being rude or snotty or not playing well, I'm going to discipline in a way that's fair.

My husband always makes fun of me. He says that you can see how much I enjoy going to a park because I walk around like I'm a security guard. I was a teacher, so I activate full-on teacher mode and use my teacher voice. I'm out there saying, "Take your turns. One at a time. We're going to do this in a fair and equitable way. Hey, who had that first? He did? Then you're next. I'm telling you, if you can't play nice, we're going to leave. And you know what? We're all here to have a good time, so be nice to each other. Go run. Green light. Red light. Green light."

If someone steps out of line, I'm on it. "You! What's your name? Where's your mom? Hi, Mom? He's crawling up the slide. There's an order to things, and he needs to get on board. 'Scuse me but your hair looks really good. Did you get it done today?"

It's like my favorite place to be. I want everybody to discipline other people's kids because it sends the message that no one's child is the most important. I'm not that big of a hippie, but I do think that maybe if we all start reminding ourselves that we aren't the most important thing in the universe, then we can all start to become more mindful of one another. Maybe it's social media, maybe it's smartphones, maybe it's just human nature, but it feels like people in general tend to feel, for lack of a better word, entitled. We're not entitled to anything. We have to coexist. Your kid isn't entitled to have first dibs at the sandbox or not share the toys when family comes over. If you have a sense of entitlement, you and I are probably not going to get along.

I totally agree with Jen that we should all help one another out. If you see that I'm struggling and you are nice enough and confident enough to ask if I need help, I'm going to let you hold my baby. That's pretty much the only checking I'm doing. I size you up and think, *Can you hold a thirty-pound time bomb? Can I run faster than you? And how bad do I have to go to the bathroom?* And I'll do the same for you.

For Colin and me, our whole thing is to lead with love, be firm, and make threats. We do *a lot* of threatening. And often zero follow-through. We feel like using our words is the right way to handle things 99 percent of the time. We are also occasional spankers. We do it if they do something that could hurt themselves or hurt another person, and we just give them a little pop on the butt, because the kids understand that language. We don't do it often, but we like to keep the threat alive. We're not gonna reason with a three-year-old who, *after thirty warnings*, keeps trying to remove the outlet covers so his toddler sister will put her finger in the socket and get zapped. (Three-year-olds: real sociopaths.)

Now that they have gotten a little older, I've found that when I'm the most honest and direct with my kids is when it has the greatest impact. We spank less and plead more. There was one time just last week when we were cleaning our house and I felt worked to death. I had just put down the mop when Finn came in from outside and stomped mud all over the floor. He knows we have a no-shoes-in-the-house rule, and he was trying to be sneaky.

I lost my mind. "Finn! Finn! What is up? You're six, you're smart, and this is an uncool move, man! And you won't clean this up, so now I'm going to have to do it. Why are you making things hard for me? You're supposed to be my teammate, and you've made it harder for me."

And he could tell I meant it. It wasn't a long speech trying to manipulate him into being a better person. It was my honest reaction, and it connected. He was so sorry. We cleaned it up together, and I feel pretty sure that next time, he'll at least knock some of the clumps off his shoes before he comes in. It really set me off, but we have rules in place to make the village not look like such a hellhole.

Look, he's six. I know I can't lecture him every time he steps out of line, so I keep it to the basics. I'll say, "Don't pee in the sandbox." Clear and simple. We'll talk about the rest later, but let's just start there, you know? And he'll go, "Yeah, okay." Discipline isn't just for the good of my kid or your kid. It's about the whole community being cool with one another. We're all just writing this book as we go, right? If we start teaching kids that we all have to get along, then maybe as adults they'll be like, "All right, I get it. We're all in the same playground. Let's not be difficult."

I DRESS FOR SUCCESS SO HARD

We don't have time to dress nice. Some days, we don't have time to dress at all. The reality is that, as a mom, you roll out of bed and make lunches, help other people put on a semi-sensible outfit, make sure nobody's breath smells like dead bird, and *maybe* change out of the pants that you slept in the last four nights.

We used to dress nice, and when we get that rare chance to go out, we have a special shirt for it. But on the daily, we wear a free T-shirt from the dentist because we know we're going to use the end of it to wipe a kid's mouth. We have even ended our relationship with shoelaces. They're too much work, and you have to bend over. Ask lots of people. Kristin, for one, is all about the Tevas. Velcro. Easy.

When we're getting dressed now, our personal style is fast, easy, and plenty of give. Which ironically was our dating profile description in our twenties. Style needs change when you become a mom. No crisp collars or tailored slacks for us anymore unless someone breaks in during the night and dresses us while we sleep. We used to put a lot of time into looking effortless, now we put no effort into looking put together.

Unlike during our twenties, we no longer read "and be sexy" into the dress code when we are invited somewhere. Jen once went to a "Caribbean Christmas" party dressed as a pirate, sporting a white blouse, a vest, and an eye patch. Everyone else read the invisible ink and showed up in flip-flops and string bikinis flossing their rumps. But guess who was the last one doing the robot and the coffee grinder on the dance floor at the end of the night, fools?

JEN

Growing up, I dressed the way your great aunt thinks gay men dress: I loved glitter, high heels, and boas, which was perfect for my anticipated future career as a *Solid Gold* dancer. (I was also a huge fan of Barbra Streisand and Barry Manilow, just to throw a little more gay stereotype into the mix.)

I needed a little extra sparkle when I was younger because I think I must have suffered from some sort of allover nerve/sensory damage as a kid. I am oblivious to a lot of things. My mom has an acute awareness of variations in color. She'll show me paint samples as she painstakingly picks a shade of eggshell that will complement her dormer: "Should I go with this one with the greenish hue or this one with the slightly mauve base?" I, on the other hand, have had eleven fender benders because I didn't register the two-ton vehicles coming at me at slow speeds. All that to say, if clothing is not shiny or brightly colored, I barely notice it.

When I was going out a lot in my twenties, it used to be, *Let me just get a spray tan, whiten my teeth, and slay.* I loved pleather and a good happy hour, but that was also the time in my life when I had to have my mom pick me up from a bar because I'd been drinking since 7:00 a.m. and couldn't find my way home. I'm not in that place anymore, thank God. Now if you asked me to do a striptease, I would most likely work the running man in. And I wouldn't wear heels to do it. Maybe character shoes, but that's it. The point is, my uniform has changed over the years, as it should, 'cause girl, so have I.

I really liked my clothes once I became a grown-ass woman with a job and a place of my own. I wore skirts and sexy lady shoes every day, and damn if I didn't look pretty put together. I even showered semi-regularly. Now I have four cans of dry shampoo in my hair, and my daywear is basically whatever I slept in plus a hoodie and a bra (sometimes). Unless I have to leave the house, that is; then I choose from my stack of stretchy pants paired with one of my five chambrays.

That said, there's nothing I wouldn't wear if I thought it was cool. Doesn't matter to me whether somebody says, "Oh, you can really see her b-hole." It's not that I really want to show off my body, but if I like something, I like it and that's it.

It drives Kristin crazy when I describe myself this way because she thinks I'm not giving myself enough style credit, but I am a pretty basic bitch. If Banana Republic thinks I should wear it, I probably think I should too, but paired with a huge rhinestone necklace. To be honest, BR is kind of upscale for me these days. I'm not into clothes with too many sharp corners. I don't buy clothes anymore unless they're from a place that also sells drain cleaner, and when I do buy clothes, it's usually a cardigan or a tank top, because layers are the utility knife of the mom uniform. Every mom's got cardigans. And hoodies. And tank tops. They're just practical. Personally, I have three levels of cardigans. The first is "Oops, I forgot to put the garbage out." These are all pilly and full of holes. I wash them in the washer and dryer just to get the dog hair off. Next I have cardigans from my "This will keep me warm and doesn't stink" pile. Those are for a big night out, like when I am going to the grocery store to pick up more Pop-Tarts. And finally there are the fancy "I got this from my in-laws at Christmas and it only has one coffee stain on the cuff—wear me to a wedding" cardigans.

Layers are the bomb because you don't always want a full-on warm jacket when you spend most of your life sweating already. A stiff ten-degree breeze feels incredible once you've spent a good twenty minutes packing everyone into a car, so you layer up and then peel down to your tank top every two hours. I have more tank tops than South Beach. I am almost always wearing one.

On the bottom, you'll find me in my "around the house" pants—even when I am most definitely not around the house. They have an elastic waistband and a nice wide seat to air out my undercarriage and give the pee leaks some runway. Underneath, I still have maternity underwear that I wear when it's not my husband's birthday. I look at my old sexy underwear and think, *Well, maybe I can find a way to Pinterest these into a cute hair tie.*

I don't wear any shoes that tie. I need to be able to slip them on with my arms full, and they need to go with everything. Extra points if I can just hose them down to clean them. Radical honesty, you guys? I've caught myself pausing in front of the Crocs kiosk at the mall. Have I given up? It's close, but I'm not totally there. Yet.

It may not help my case when I tell you that anytime we're at a casino and there's an old lady at the slots drinking coffee in a velour tracksuit, my husband will say, "You want to be her, don't you?" He may think I'm styling myself after the grannie set because, like all the cool moms, I've got readers. And no, they're not the ones with ironic chunky frames from Warby Parker; they're the ones with the decidedly unironic chunky frames from the endcap at Walgreens.

Despite the questionable footwear and eyewear, I do love a good bag. Kristin's purse is essentially a leather fanny pack. My makeup bag is the size of her entire purse. I like a bag that's big enough that my chiropractor gets excited when he sees me wearing it. He takes one look and thinks, *Ka-ching! I'll be seeing you weekly for the next six years.* My current bag weighs approximately a third of what I do. I've actually wondered if I could fit my daughter in it. I just need a monster bag. It is very difficult to fit wipes, ten different kinds of gummies, water bottles, a change of clothes for each kid, and a full box of tampons in a cute little clutch. I found quiche in my bag one time. Okay, it might have been frittata, but there was egg and spinach in it for sure. Anyway, it was definitely not something you'd find in a YSL satchel.

You've got to wear clothes that work for what you are all about. I still like to have a good time—just like in my twenties!—it just happens that my good times occur during the day now, and they maybe require a little more give around the waist. My good times don't have to be quality, high-maintenance affairs with a lot of planning (this may be how my husband describes our love life, as I am lazy). I love singing too loud in the car with the kids, making an old man laugh at the grocery store, and overdecorating for the holidays—any holiday—and I don't need to be in a halter to enjoy any of that. But that doesn't stop me from buying halters anyway.

I feel like you should wear what you love, or at least feel comfortable in, because you're the one who has to deal with it all day. I will buy an impractical shoe if I think it will make me happy to look down at my feet. I pretty much tell my kids the same thing. As long as it passes as clean, I let them wear it. Delilah loves a good princess gown and cowboy boot ensemble, and so does my son. I'm fine with it, because those items give them joy and make them feel like the best version of themselves. I really believe in buying some signature pieces for yourself. They don't even have to be expensive, but they should remind you who you are as a mom and as a human. The "as a human" part is so important because during those early years, especially when you *first* become a mom, your body belongs to somebody else. Not only that, but it's like suddenly your life belongs to someone else, and that's a hard thing to get your head around.

I really felt that way when I was breastfeeding. I hate to admit it, but I was pretty excited when I quit breastfeeding because I don't like button-down shirts. I had to wear them all the time so my boobs were easily accessible, and I prefer something that zips up the back. A nice jumpsuit, maybe. It felt symbolically important when I could wear what I wanted to again, so yeah, I will buy a sequined top if I think it will brighten my day.

I'm not sure Kristin has ever donned a single item of clothing with reflective properties. I love her style—sort of rock 'n' roll meets sensible shoes—but I feel like she's constantly on the verge of doubling down on the Tevas with sport socks and the fanny pack. So I like to do all of her shopping for her.

KRISTIN

Jen shops like it's a sport. She stays skinny because when she shops she hits her target heart rate. I know there are many reasons she loves me, but one of the big ones is that after Delilah, I'm her favorite girl to buy clothes for. And for the most part, I wear everything she picks out for me. She delights in coordinating and accessorizing, so I let her. I need the help because I'm not a very good shopper. If you ask me if I want to go shopping with you, I'll say, "Why? Am I being punished?"

Every time Jen leaves her house, she comes back loaded with bags for me. She comes over, says, "I thought this would look really good on you," and then spills a sale rack full of stuff onto my couch. She doesn't even let me go with her because I get bored so easily and she doesn't like to feel rushed. And she doesn't shop just for me. She shops for my kids too. I'll be in the middle of making lunches and I'll get a call: "What's Finn's shoe size now?"

It's probably for the best because going into dressing rooms is my living nightmare. I shouldn't feel this bad about myself. I'm a size 10. That is a perfectly reasonable size, you guys. My doctors tell me, "Kristin, you're so healthy it's dumb," but then I get into a fitting room and suddenly I want to punch gravity in the face. When did my butt turn into one huge field of cellulite? When did I get permanent back-fat folds? Can't gravity just flip the script and start pulling things upward instead? If I could just walk around upside down, I'd be so hot.

It's difficult to choose what to wear because so many things just make you feel terrible about yourself, especially if you let yourself care what other people think, and when I was a kid I cared hard.

Fashion was pretty terrible when I was growing up, but it made my parents' life so easy. When I look back at photos of me in the nineties, I do not feel bad for them at all. For once. What, they had to warn me, "Kristin, stop wearing your dad's oversize flannel with your baggy jeans and combat boots. It's too revealing." Ha. Now girls that age are wearing shorts so short that they look like a swim diaper. Girls are dressing more sophisticated at twelve than I did at . . . well, ever.

I hope my daughter has the balls to make her own calls when it comes to how she dresses. What I really hope is that a real strong *Downton Abbey* look is big when my daughter is in middle school. Lots of buttons, collars, hair pulled back, maybe an English accent. Most of all, I want her to ignore what other people want her to wear and just do her own thing. I didn't.

Back when I was in sixth grade or so, I bought a really cool shirt that looked like it came from the set of *Blossom*. It was a real fashion risk for small-town Central City. It had a lot of daring ruffles. It was one of the most expensive shirts I'd ever bought, and I loved it. But all it took was my annoying cousin James to make one shitty comment, and I never wore it again. I wanted to say, "I don't give a monkey's butt about what you think, James. I love this shirt, and I am going to wear it." But I wasn't that person then—and getting to be that person was a journey.

I've come to terms with who I am and how I am when it comes to my own personal style. I love a good pair of jeans, a T-shirt, and a cool pair of tennis shoes. Jen says my style is "modern comfort," and I definitely think comfort is sexy, but I will be the first to admit that sometimes comfy is a slippery slope into cargo shorts and free T-shirts.

I can pretty much figure out my day-to-day style just fine (jeans, T-shirt, nice kicks). I've got that down pat, but when it comes to business meetings or "fancy stuff," I break into a cold sweat. I tend to do it wrong no matter how hard I try.

I mean, I had a fit about our shoot for this book cover. I was going to splurge at Bloomingdale's because I thought if I bought something nice I'd feel amazing and hot and like I belonged on the cover of a book. But after trying on a ton of stuff, nice stuff, I bummed out. I kept saying, "This isn't right. Damn. Neither is this. This would look so awesome if . . . ," and I had this sinking realization that nothing was going to make me feel good because I was still fifteen pounds over. I had that crappy "You can't put lipstick on a pig" feeling.

I try to remind myself that everybody is a work in progress. You gotta give yourself a break. You know how they say, "If you wait till the perfect time to have a baby, you'll never have a baby"? If you wait till you look your best to buy nice clothes, you'll end up butt naked.

Jen is really good about this. Her attitude is "I don't care if this looks good on me. I wanna wear it because it has sparkles on it." Sometimes she doesn't even try stuff on because if she likes it, she's going to wear it anyway. When I hear her say that, I am so impressed, but it's hard for me to get there all the time.

Because of #IMOMSOHARD, we have had the chance to do some really cool stuff. We've traveled the country doing comedy, we've been on TV, and we've even walked the red carpet. I will tell you, if there is one thing that will make you quickly figure out what you like and don't like about yourself, it's seeing yourself wearing something dumb and knowing you'll be sashaying down a path where everyone else can see it too.

One of the awesome things we got to do was go to a movie premiere. Sounds cool, right? I was very excited at first—until I realized I was going to have to figure out what to wear. For like five minutes, I thought I was saved because the company that invited us provided a stylist, someone who picks out clothes for you and brings them to your home so you can try them on before an event. Again, sounds cool, right?

It's f*cking awful.

The stylist was a twig, and she was not happy to be dressing someone "plus size" like me. (Apparently, double digits equals "plus size.") I'm perfectly average size. It shouldn't be that hard. She brought in one rack of clothes that were very loud and very bedazzled. They looked like dresses the mother of the bride would have worn to a wedding in the eighties. One had a bow on the shoulder that covered part of my face. It was hard not to take that personally. The stylist had to come back the next day because I was so hard to fit.

I've never felt so ashamed. How big am I? Are fancy clothes reserved for the thin? That stylist looked at me like she was trying to fit a pretty dress onto a dumpster. Am I supposed to wear a caftan? WTF?

Anyway, we went to the event. We walked the red carpet. I hated everything I was wearing. They put me in a high-waisted black jumpsuit with shiny buttons and wide legs. It made me look pregnant, and it really highlighted my camel toe. It just wasn't for me. I had on so much makeup and such a dark orange fake tan that I looked like the real housewives of the suburbs. I didn't like myself. But the good news is, when we walked the red carpet nobody knew who we were. The photographers would literally put down their cameras when we walked by. A win! There were no pictures to document my night! Lesson learned. Next time we get invited to a red carpet (please let there be a next time), I'm going to just do me.

I do have one item that I know will make me feel like a million bucks every time I put it on. I paid a lot of money for it, and I have no problem saying that because I work really hard. It's a leather motorcycle jacket that now has two giant holes in it, but I feel so like me when I have it on. It's like my uniform that I wear to the job of being me.

I love when I see ladies who are owning their style, like the Hispanic women in my Zumba class. I love the way Latina women dress there because they are not size 0s. If they're full figured, and they're still pushing up their boobs and wearing

205

their favorite things, they feel feminine because they're leading with the things they like about themselves—boobs, butt, whatever. They're not gonna stop feeling hot, even if they have a little extra in the middle. I've been trying to channel that inner *chica* recently.

Every once in a while, it works. Something about being a mom has kicked my "f*ck 'em" attitude up at least one notch. Maybe it's the fact that I'm not going to wear a tube top because it's not my top that needs tubing—it's more like I need to tube my middle. Or maybe it's that when you spend more than a tenth of your day touching someone else's poop, you learn fast that trying to look perfect or hot all the time is insane. Making a freaking life and then raising it to be a person in the world? That throws other people's opinions about your shirt into perspective. Now I'm going to wear a shirt that says "I just burped" on the front and "I just farted" on the back, and I'm going to feel good about it, dammit.

These days, I'm dressing for me, for my life. I've gotten more comfortable in my own skin since becoming a mom. I'm going for effortless and easy to move in. Costco is where I buy my fruit, my poultry, my porch lights, and my jeans. My husband bought me fancy (slutty) stuff from Victoria's Secret, and it still has the price tag on it. Then he bought me long underwear from Victoria's Secret, and I've worn a hole in it. (Not there. Gross, you guys.)

I felt sexy and powerful in my clothes when I went hiking in Yosemite earlier this year. I had my hiking hat on, my flannel, and my hiking boots, and I was with my kids. I thought, *I can dominate this right now. This is my jam. This is one place*

I can just be me. My beard is 100 percent acceptable in the mountains.

I choose my outfit based on whether it's smores-ready or not. I'm trying to have a good time with my kids. I'm no longer seeking that thing a man does where he looks over his sunglasses at you appreciatively like he's the bad boy in a Brat Pack movie. I'm trying not to ruin my good times by worrying about whether my vibe is sexy.

Recently, I went to my daughter's graduation from preschool. Eleanor loves when I wear dresses, so I wore the *one* summery dress I own with pink flats and a matching purse. Nailed it! We are new at the school, so I wanted to make a good impression. We were invited to an after party, and I was buzzing with delight, but first I went home and changed because the invite said it was a barbecue. I changed out of my dress, put on my funniest Willy Nelson T-shirt, cutoff shorts, and Nikes, because I thought it was casual—that we'd be dressing down to play with our kids—and then I got there and it turned out that I was the only mom who did a wardrobe change. Everyone else still had on their dresses.

I felt like crap for a little bit and then I decided, *You know what? I'm gonna make everybody else feel better because I clearly did it wrong.* And you know what happened? I got down with some rosé and I *owned* that party. By the time I left, I think those moms were saying, "Man, why did I wear this stupid floral shift dress when I could have worn a Willie Nelson shirt?"

I DO SEXY STUFF SO HARD

Before kids, when you have sex, every position you put your body in feels like you are modeling for a centerfold. It's all very exciting. In the beginning, there is the thrill of the chase followed by hour-long make-out sessions. Then you finally do *it* . . . and eventually you decide to become a couple, and then you do it *a bunch*. Every way you lie down on the bed, the sheets end up between your legs in a sexy way, and your butt's propped up. You're always doing fun messy hair. Everything's just where it needs to be. Ladies, you feel sexy, amiright?

And then after you have kids, you lie in bed and you look like a cadaver. Your legs are flopped open, you instantly fall asleep with "soft jaw" (that's when your mouth is partially open so it gently slides back and gives you seven chins), you're on a weird breastfeeding pillow, and there's always a faint smell of poop. No one even knows if you're breathing. Maybe no one even cares. You do *not* feel sexy.

It's not that moms don't enjoy sex. It's just that it's a real time commitment. It feels like you shelved your libido and you couldn't find it if you wanted to behind all the crap in your way, like buying diapers and scrubbing dried peas out of your yoga pants. It takes a while to get back into the swing of things. Married sex isn't terrible. It's just unimpressive.

Married sex is all about "How do we get from point A to point *Oohhh* to point *Zzz* and still have time to watch *House Hunters*?" With kids and schedules and filling our Amazon cart, mom life is a perpetual game of playing hard to get. As in, when you are a mom you hardly get it.

We moms don't have enough room in our brains to think about sex. Even if the opportunity arises (*ba dom ching!*), our brains take us out of it. *Is today show-and-tell? Is that my stomach fat I feel lying on the bed? Do I still have a gym membership? If I could only remember my email password. Did I drop that permission slip off at my kid's school?* But you know you didn't. You know it's at the bottom of your mom bag. Aaaaaaaand there goes your good time.

It's easy to find yourself in a sex drought, with your partner very, very thirsty. Our husbands come up to us and say, "Hey, uh, you know, it's been two weeks . . . ," and we'll respond, "Nope, sorry, buddy. It's only been thirteen days. You're fine." We have needs too—they just don't always get to the top of the list above fulfilling the needs of *every other person in the house*. But it's not a lost cause. You just need the right approach, gentlemen. If you want to visit our lady gardens, you should know we are not that complex—we just have different turn-ons.

If you want sex to happen, then help with a little housework—maybe hang up some towels—and don't say stupid shit just before go time. That's it. Plus, wine helps. Our husbands have a 30 percent greater chance of getting some action if we drink wine.

KRISTIN

I was late to the sex game. I didn't give up my virginity until I was twenty-one. I was such a late arrival that my friend Brandy bought me balloons at the Dollar Store that said "Congratulations!" when it finally happened. I made up for lost time, though—by which I mean I did my twenties right.

And then I fell in love with my husband.

I knew Colin was perfect for me the day we met. I looked into his eyes and said, "This is the first time I've ever dated anyone with facial hair," and he looked back at me and said, "Me too."

When you first start dating someone, it's all humping and appetizers. Everything is about passion. Sex *always* sounds like a good idea. Colin and I wore a hole in the bed, and the chairs, and the kitchen counter, and even the back seat of my MINI Cooper.

My husband set the stage for how our sex life would play out almost immediately. During those early months, I was still teaching and had to be at school at 8:13 a.m., and he would always want to start fooling around at 7:55. I'd be in bed and he'd start poking me with his boner, and I'd tell him, "I have four seconds until I have to go teach high school and not smell like sex, so this has to happen fast." And he'd ask, "How fast?" I'd say, "You have three minutes." He'd reply with gusto, "Mark it." He's very task oriented.

Right after you get married, even if you're not in the mood, you can always be talked into it. It might take a sec to get the ball rolling, but once it does, hang on because just-married sex is great. He's figured out what you like—and when to open the bedside table drawer. You've got the relationship on lock now, so you don't have to show off. Those days are done. You already did the work to impress him a long time ago. Plus, you publicly, legally, and metaphorically shouted from the rooftops, "I choose to hump this person until I die." There's something really freeing about that. You don't have to feel shy about asking for what you want. You can yell at him, "Get on the other side of me! We both know you're left-handed!" That's intimacy.

But after a few years go by, things can, and probably will, change. Instead of getting busy every chance you get, you say, "If I have sex with you, will you finally plant those freaking bougainvillea?" Or "If I do this, will you finish the fence, for the love of God? What do I have to do to get you to do this one thing?" And then you do one thing in return. Because that's fair. You're not trying to win any medals.

We had kids really early in our marriage—as in, the priest said, "Do you, Colin, take this woman who is trying to convincingly hide a five-month pregnancy to be your companion forever and ever and ever? Hahahahahahaha."

So I learned right away that, post-kids, moms don't just do it for fun. Everyone is in survival mode. You sleep in different rooms. You shower alone (if at all). There's no romance besides a wink and a fond glance that says, "Oh, yeah. I remember you." And there's a lot of negotiation that has to happen before anybody's getting it on. You have to set realistic expectations about the next five minutes. You figure out what everybody has the emotional and physical stamina for. It's just like any job: you need to establish parameters to prevent scope creep.

I'm not trying to be complainy about my husband. I love him. It's the situation, not the man.

I'm sure there are fancy therapists and love doctors who have really eloquent ways of describing intimacy in a marriage. I'm not a doctor. My husband and I high-five after we make love. That's who we are. The way I see it, after you're married, your sex life becomes less like you're living a romance novel and more like you're assembling Ikea furniture. While at first it's all very complicated, you know as time passes you will have built something together. And because you built it together, you know where the weak spots are, and you can live with the scuffs and scratches that come with time and understanding.

Somehow, even though I know he is just as tired and overwhelmed as I am, Colin is still always up for gettin' down. I don't need to make any moves. I just sigh, "Okay." If I actually express interest? Game *on*. I could literally say, "Hey, do you want to—" and his pants are off. I have this one shirt that's like a green light if I put it on. I know I'm getting some action. It's my husband's college T-shirt; it says "Texas A&M." I know. NSFW, right?

These days, the kids take priority 98 percent of the time, but we do slot sex in every once in a while. A few weeks ago, we put on some *PAW Patrol* and then ran back into the bedroom and got to business right away. When we looked up, both of our kids were standing in the door like, *What are you doing?* Naturally, I told them we were just arguing lying down. And the kids said, "Oh, okay," and went back to Chase and Ryder (why have we never noticed how dirty the character names in *PAW Patrol* are?). And then I cried because I had ruined them forever.

I know because it ruined *me* when I walked in on my parents. Every week after Sunday school they would tell me to go change out of my church clothes and then go play outside for thirty minutes and *DO NOT COME BACK IN THE HOUSE NO MATTER WHAT YOU HEAR.* When we'd come back in, they'd be in these weird terry-cloth robes and matching slippers, my mom in ducks, my dad in mallards. I'd wonder, *What exactly is going on here in this den of sin?* (I'd just come from church, so I was talking like Jim Bakker.) Despite all the warnings, I walked in on them in the act when I was fourteen. When the door flew open, they both turned their heads left and they were both looking at me. At the time I thought they were just playing leap frog. It was mortifying. Afterward, my mom wanted to talk about it—ya know, a teachable moment kinda thing: "Now, Kristin, it's very natural. Your father and I are in love, and it's what married people do." My dad just said, "Next time, knock." *That's* the conversation I wanted to have.

My kids clearly felt the same way. When Colin and I got busted, the next day my kids didn't ask any questions or follow up at all. In fact, they were 100 percent uninterested, which sort of hurt my feelings, if I'm honest about it. Was it so bad it didn't even look a *little* bit like fun? Was I so *meh* that they thought, *Whatever you and Daddy were doing, it looked super boring*? Who knows, though maybe it will work to our benefit because if they're ever tempted to get busy in their teen years, they'll think, *That didn't look like any fun. Let's play Xbox Nine instead.*

I'm hopeful that things will pick up a bit when the kids are older and more self-sufficient. A few months ago, we had some friends over, and they have a son, an only child, who's much older than our kids. Our friend was bragging, "Yeah, we're having kind of a sexual renaissance. We're back in it. We're really enjoying each other." So there's hope. But in the moment, I looked at Colin and said, "We race to the bed just to see who doesn't have to be on top." And that's God's honest truth. We sprint to the bedroom to see who can rip off their clothes the fastest and get in the bed and lie on their back and say, "No, I don't want to be on top. My back hurts. I don't want to do it. You do it."

I do think about what kind of sex life we're modeling for the kids. Is that creepy? What I want them to know, especially my daughter, is that it's the intimacy that matters, because that's when you're able to focus on really connecting. So many of us girls had early sexual experiences just because we were trying to attain some sort of relationship or trying to gain status. I want Eleanor to know that she is in charge of her own happiness. I want her to have the attitude, *If you get a key to the kingdom, it's because you know my favorite ska band*, not *I have to do this because then he'll like me*. That makes me feel sick.

My biggest fear is that she'll end up with someone because she feels like she has to couple up or that she'll end up without someone because she doesn't feel good enough. Both of those are terrible. I just want her to know herself, love herself, and have experiences that don't require a boyfriend: travel, study, paint, whatever. And then when she chooses her mate, I hope she'll have a relationship that is rich, loving, and full of joy and humor.

What I want most for Finn is for him to understand that intimacy comes from taking the time to really get to know a gal. When he finds a girl he likes, we want our son to open doors, to pick up the check, to help her study for the MCAT (fingers crossed on that one). He'll urge her to sing her folk music at an open mic. He'll leave her love notes, let her choose the movie, and dance with her anywhere he can. He'll hold her hand, and when they argue he will *never* call her a bitch. (By that time, surveillance will be so easy that I will be able to pop him in the mouth from outer space.) And he should expect the same—a girl who makes his interests her interests, who lets him be sad or cranky or quiet if he needs to be, and who takes real delight in who he is, not what he can do for her. Someday, when they are much older, and when the time is NEVER right, I will struggle through an honest conversation with each of my kids about sex. I'll blink a lot, pause often, clear my throat, look to my husband for help, and I'll pray for the strength to make the point that sex is intimate and should be something that both of you enjoy and it should be reserved for those who you know and love. And then I will leave abruptly and pour myself a huge glass of wine.

My parents talked to me about sex, but they didn't get into details. Not me. I will absolutely get into details with my kids. For now, at their young age, the details are just about teaching both of our kids how to "trust their gut." Jen once told me that one of my best qualities as a mom is that I am trying to teach my kids to trust their instincts. I constantly tell them, "Hey, if your stomach feels weird around someone, then you walk away or come tell Mommy." We have conversations about how no one is allowed to touch their privates *ever*, and how when they choose to, ahem, touch their own privates, that it's natural and normal and important, *but* they have to go in the other room because it's inappropriate to do that while watching *Henry Danger*. We don't force them to hug *anybody*, but we encourage fist bumps and high fives. Once they are older, we will give them details about sex. The nitty-gritty. The real deal. I pray we have the courage to talk right through it instead of around it: "Have fun—and remember if you have sex you could contract a life-threatening STD!" "Call me when you get to the party, and don't put your penis in anyone if they have been drinking!" "Blue balls aren't real, and boners go away. Enjoy the movie!" I just want them to respect themselves and opt for a relationship instead of giving it up in the back of a Kia.

Even when you're young and everything's hot and passionate, intimacy is the game changer, but it becomes even more important over the long haul. Listen, it's not easy to feel sexy sometimes. I've literally checked out of my own fantasy and given up because I thought Khal Drogo wouldn't be into me anyway, so what's the point? You've felt this way, right? It's hard to feel good about your body as a mother and as an older woman. I wish we wouldn't be so hard on ourselves, but we are, which is why, when you have someone you can trust to love all of you—who holds you when you're having a vulnerable moment and feel like you're a bad mom and you're doing everything wrong—it gives you the confidence to know you're lovable and maybe even, in the right light, *very lovable*. Besides, sex for all men, really, is great. They're happy to get it. He doesn't care what size you are, he just cares that your vagina is attached. If we go up two pounds we feel like, "Oh, everything fits differently. I'm so unattractive." Yeah, well, your vagina still fits, and believe me, that is his favorite thing to wear.

I feel very fortunate to be married to a man who gets me. I'm difficult, short-tempered, and fragile, and my self-confidence has its peaks and valleys. To him, I'm pretty great. And being with him physically is fun and silly. That's what's awesome about doing it with someone who has seen you at your worst—when you're covered in puke and poop and haven't showered in days and your crotch should have caution tape around it—and yet he would still bone you. You trust him. You know he's not in it just for a few minutes of rubbing, but for a lifetime.

You can't always make your love life one all-inclusive package. Sometimes, you knock one out in the hall closet—because you've only got three minutes, ain't nobody got time for sweet nothings—and then the intimacy comes later when you're sitting across from each other having a glass of wine. Then there are those rare moments when you find yourself in the throes of a steamy sex session and you get equally turned on by the act and by how you've still got it. Those are the times when you look over at your hubby and get all weird and girlie for a couple of days. That's when we can say all the nice stuff. I feel like the most important part of our marriage is honesty, and I'm very honest with my husband about sex. In fact, I always say my dream sex life would be if my husband would just go load the dishwasher, I could sort of take care of my business, and by the time he gets back we can take care of his business and we'll be done in seven minutes and can watch Netflix. Then we can have a nice chat about our feelings. This usually includes my husband looking at me and saying, "God, I like you so much more after we do this." And then we laugh and high-five.

JEN

You know that saying, "Sex is like pizza: even bad pizza can still be good, and even bad sex is still good"? That's correct for men. That is *not* correct for women. For women, that pizza is not giving you an orgasm. In fact, it might be giving you the clap. And it didn't even taste good. It wasn't fully cooked. It burned the roof of your mouth so you get that dangly skin for a few days, constantly reminding you that you shouldn't have dived into the pizza so quickly. You should have thought about it first. Besides, that pizza was gross, like from a Pizza Shuttle, and you should have waited until you could find something gourmet, from a sit-down restaurant with a stone hearth that doesn't creep you out by saying "make love." You know that guy's gonna want to wash your hair or go antique shopping. Wait . . .

Now that I am married, you would think I would be eating that gourmet pizza six nights a week, and I consider my husband to be like a Wolfgang Puck, but like Kristin said, the reality is that sex slips down the priority list after the kids show up. The first thing you need to do if you want to get it on when you have kids is find the right time of day for it. For some reason, the morning is the best time for men. That is the stinkiest, worst-breath time of the day for me. I usually have pillow creases in my face that last for an hour or so—and often a surprise ruin-your-school-photos pimple. You're trying to shake off the Sleep of the Mom, which is basically the Sleep of the Dead. Waking up from a three-month coma might be the only time you would feel grosser and less inclined to bone. Not to mention that you're so busy in the morning. If you add sex to the morning routine, something else falls off the list—like tooth brushing or putting on pants. Every time I show up to work in a ponytail, everybody knows what's up. Coworkers raise their eyebrows. *Fun morning, huh?*

Nighttime is hard too, though. You're so wiped by the time you've fed everybody, bathed everybody, and gotten them into bed, and then you've still got a whole lot of online shopping that you want to get done. Then you have to check social media and gauge your failures against everyone else's remodeled kitchens. It just doesn't leave a lot of time for sex. And yet you'll be in the middle of bedtime routine mania and your husband will turn to you and say, "Come on. The kids are brushing their teeth. Just for a second!" It's never a second. It's eleven minutes and carpal tunnel syndrome. I don't have time for a medical injury. I know he's into it, but if I get into it, we're committed. It becomes a whole night-long ordeal where I'll want to cuddle and have "We should go to an island, just you and me" conversations, and that's no good for anybody. We work in the morning and someone will be running into the bedroom at 5:00 a.m. anyway.

However, there *is* a sex window for women. It's usually just after watching a steamy scene on HBO, having a half glass of wine too much, taking a shower, and then waiting too long to get dressed. You can actually look at yourself in the mirror and think, *Hey, nipples! I don't look like a blow-up doll, but if I squint, I have all the right parts to feel good about.* You feel a slight breeze of "Oh, yeah, I kind of . . ." blow across your lady parts. That's when I like to put on a robe real loose-like and say something super seductive like "Hey, what's your wiener doing?" I'm not well versed in the language of love (I mean, the self-help kind I'm fluent in, obviously), but luckily, my husband speaks my language.

I agree with Kristin. I think sex is actually better after you're married and have kids, because you just get to it and your whole goal is "How do we make each other feel good so we're less difficult to be around, and everybody's a little happier, and stuff gets done?" Even if I'm totally wiped, I know that everybody's better off if we do it, even if it's been a little bit of a dry spell. You gotta get in there, just get the ball rolling, and then everything starts to feel good. Just get the party started. With the slightest bit of encouragement—like twenty minutes' worth—you're *so* on board. I'm not saying you have to do a halftime show, gentlemen, but a little pregaming goes a long way. And then, odds are, I'm going to remember that good time for several nights and maybe even ask for a three-peat before we slump back into the "It's been about a month" doldrums.

Life, man. It gets in the way of fun stuff all the time. My husband and I have this way that we say "good night" to each other, and we both know what it means. I say, "Good night. I love you." But my intonation says, "I'm possibly going to die in my sleep because today killed me. I would hump the crap out of you if I had any energy left in my legs." Then I rub his shoulder as if to say, "Imagine if this were your dong, and I did it more aggressively for ten minutes. I used to be fun."

It's not our husbands. It's life.

But sometimes it *is* our husbands.

Example: Early in my relationship with Brit, I told him I had something to ask him. He put down his phone and looked up, and I asked, "Do you think we're already in love?" He was quiet for a second and then he said, "I thought you were going to ask if you could give me a hand job." What woman asks that?! What man says no? You never ask! They never say no. You could be in the middle of the school parking lot and they're like, "Hey, you should touch it for a little bit. Don't waste it."

In the beginning, you totally overlook their flaws. And then you have kids, and their flaws come rushing back. Maybe we'd be up for it a little more often than almost never, but men handicap themselves. They say the wrong things. They say dumb things.

Again, an example: The other night, I was sitting with my husband, trying to tell him something that made me feel really vulnerable, and his response was "Do you remember a show called *Battle of the Network Stars*?" No, I don't. And if this is dirty talk, it's terrible. Also, I was saying words that I think you didn't hear. Guess if we had sex. (We didn't.)

Sometimes I'll think, *Oh, man, it'd be nice to hug my husband, but I don't want him to get the wrong idea.* I worry that when I wear yoga pants or when I bend over to pick something up in the kitchen, he'll think it's go time. That's not how I send signals. I'm not telling you to steal home. I'm not even telling you to go for a double. I'm trying to make lunches. I'm telling you I'll Karate Kid you if you go for a bunt to first base. The reason I'm not wearing a bra is that it felt too hard to put one on, not because I'm trying to look like a Lita Ford poster.

Let's put it this way: you're not lighting candles and playing Enya. You're making each other feel good as fast as you can, and then winking at each other throughout the day. The intimacy you have in marriage is not about the sex you have in marriage; it's much deeper than that. And the tenderness and the love that you have comes out in different ways.

Cirque du Soleil sex is not where the closeness happens. It happens in the shared moments of a day when you roll your eyes behind your kids' backs or send funny text messages—like when Brit sent me a picture of some poop he found on our rug because he wanted to know whether I thought it looked like it came from a kid or the dog. Or when he sent me a photo of himself wearing special glasses and headgear because he was getting his teeth bleached.

Now, *that's* hot.

I WORK OUT
MY ISSUES
SO HARD

We all have a fitness friend, the one who delivers her baby and is like, "Phew. Just made it. Only two hours till spin class." We are not that friend. We will not call you and ask you what your VO$_2$ max is or if you've tried Orangetheory Fitness. We *will* call and ask you what your favorite show to binge-watch is or whether you think banana-flavored candy is gross. (It is, but we will eat it anyway.) Working out never feels like the thing we want to do. Kind of like sex. Moms' lives are too much like a marathon every single day for us to train for an actual marathon.

We know, we know. If we would just make time for a quick workout—*even a quick walk around the block!*—we'd feel so much better. You know what else makes us feel better? Cupcakes and a *Fixer Upper* marathon.

But there are some things that even butter and shiplap can't help with. We've both had our struggles with mental health—and we think it's important to talk about it. We tend to say, "Oh, everything's great," even when we're in pain and suffering. Instead, why don't we just say how we feel in that moment? "You know what? It's not going great. I've got a kid who throws tantrums all the time. I can't stop crying, day in and day out. I feel like I'm sinking." We are proof that once you are brave and tell the truth, people will say, "Yeah, I feel like that too." Maybe we can start changing the conversation and begin eroding the stigma and getting a little more real with one another. It's that whole "sunshine is the best disinfectant" theory, right?

JEN

If you can take care of your whole person—if you can work out, read books, have "me" time, attend to your spiritual side—and you have a clean house and your husband and kids don't hate you, my hat's off to you and I'll take whatever pill you're taking. (Wait. *Is* there a pill? I would take that. I'm serious. Text me the Rx.) But for me, a few things are going to have to suffer—and by that I mean my abs and both my thighs. Working out is just not a priority for me. I would *consider* working out for the mental health benefits. But physically, folks, this is what you're getting. You don't have to look if you don't want to.

Kristin has always been an athlete, a physical person, so she knows what her body feels like when it's in top shape. I've never been what anyone would call a jock. When I was a kid, I wasn't even allowed to do sports because my mom thought they weren't ladylike. When I see pictures of Kristin dressed for her Little League games with her rat tail hanging out from under her baseball cap, I think my mom might have been onto something. Kidding! (Full disclosure: I had a rat tail too; I think they issued them on the first day of middle school in the Midwest.) But gym class brought down my GPA, and I really missed out on the whole philosophy behind physical fitness.

I have to admit I have a bad attitude when people tell me that I need to work working out into my day. I see people constantly posting on Instagram about how great they feel after working out, writing nonsense like "AMRAP! #WOD! Who's with me?" You're telling me that in order to be my best self I need to hold a plank for two minutes? How about this? You want to improve yourself? Quit being so naggy about exercise.

I get that it makes you healthier—really, I do—but I read a lot of self-help books and that has to count for something. My brain's healthy, right? (I also read a lot of serial killer books, so then again, maybe not.)

It's not like I've never tried. I went to a spin class one time, but I didn't like it when the instructor yelled at me. I thought, *Hey, you work for me. Don't yell at me.* I don't want to stand up on the bike or go uphill. I want to stop off for a doughnut.

Kristin invited me to a barre class. I thought that sounded like something I'd like. It turns out this barre class was a workout and had all these different positions. No, thank you. I happen to be well versed in BAR positions! Mine go like this:

FIRST POSITION

Hey, everybody! I'm excited to be here! Sit down.
Order your favorite.

SECOND POSITION

Drinks on me! Lean on bar to catch bartender's attention
with your cleavage. (Modification: if over thirty or mother
of more than one child, do that thing where you wave
your credit card like a douchey banker.)

THIRD POSITION

Hey, can I tell you something? Start getting emotional.
Clutch friend's arm. Confess that you think you're a bad
mom and that you sometimes google "starting over with
a new identity" while you're supposed to be working.
Tell ghost stories. Buy stuff online.

FOURTH POSITION

Super nice you called me an Uber. Drunkenly hug your
friends or anyone nearby.

FIFTH POSITION

Floor ('cause that's where I am). This position means my
husband is bringing me a blanket when I pass out in
front of the TV.

Then Kristin explained what barre class actually is, and I
told her I would rather wear performance fleece every day for
the rest of my life than go to that. I just don't think classes are
my thing. I got kicked out of a yoga class once for laughing at
somebody queefing. Come on. You would need abs of steel not
to laugh at that. God.

The last time I went to a gym, the check-in guy said, "Hope you're taking it easy in there," as he nodded at my midsection. When it dawned on me what he meant, I turned around and shouted at him, "I'M NOT PREGNANT!!!!!!" and then never went back. It's cool. I don't need a gym membership anyway. What I need is a time machine to zap me back to when I was twenty-three and could drink all night, eat a second dinner at Carl's Jr., and show up to work the next day in my skinny jeans.

That said, there are some things that can motivate me to get moving. If you work out, you can eat more because you burn more calories, so what I like to do is get a real embarrassing playlist on my phone and then have a dance party, just me and Taylor Swift. It's a guilty pleasure. I will also hit an outlet mall and go three or four miles, and on arm day, I pour more in my glass. The more you lift, the more of a burn you get. This is just a taste of my active lifestyle.

In general, I don't like sweating, and exercise makes you sweat. You get boob sweat, you get butt sweat—I feel like those should be my dry areas, you know? If I need to sweat, I'll take both kids to the grocery store by myself.

I did once participate in a walk for an HIV/AIDS fund-raiser, but I got like two miles in and decided that while I was walking, I might as well walk to a nice brunch spot. I never finished the walk. I had already donated all the money and stuff, so don't judge me.

I seriously do not understand why I am not more ripped even though I don't go to a gym or take classes. I curl twenty-five pounds every five minutes when I'm pulling my daughter out of the dog dish or away from the toaster oven. I must do four hundred reps a day. And it's not just lifting; it's lifting and convulsing, like a compound exercise. It should be better than burpees. I don't do burpees, but I do do a lot of burping. Okay, I did try burpees with a trainer once, but I thought I was having a heart attack and started crying. Truth.

I have struggled most of my life with anxiety and depression. I wish I were one of those people who could solve it with exercise. I know those people, and they *do* seem really happy. It's just not the solution for me. My husband is fairly emotionally aware. He loves to have cupcakes and champagne and talk about feelings. But he has not had depression, he didn't grow up with anybody who had it, and he just doesn't understand it. He's one of those people who will say, "Maybe the gym would help?" His heart was in the right place, but I felt like *Oh, okay, so now there's another thing I could do that I'm just not doing?* I'm lazy now? Add that to the list. Let me stop you before you suggest that I get up before the kids and work out. Don't make me hurt you.

I was in my midtwenties when I first went to a doctor because I realized it wasn't normal to sleep an hour and a half each night and to get up at 4:00 a.m. to make sure I didn't leave my checkbook in the car. It has taken me many counselors and multiple medications to get my low lows and frantic highs to settle down. I've blamed situations, choices, people, and even myself in an attempt to give a reason for my sadness.

Here's what I discovered: for me, it's as simple as a chemical imbalance. I take Prozac, and now my thoughts don't spiral out of control like they used to. It works for me, and I have no shame about it. Some people have bad knees; I have bad serotonin. I'm not pushing drugs, but I've found that advice like "Work out, read books, get a new job" doesn't help with clinical depression.

It wasn't always easy for me to be so up-front about it. I understand why other people might not want to discuss it. You think, *Oh, if I reveal that I get depressed easily, then everything about me is going to be seen through that lens.* It's like the way you feel when somebody says, "Oh, you've got your period right now. I see. Nothing you say can be trusted." No one wants to be defined by depression or by whatever their struggle is. You're all these wonderful things that have nothing to do with that, and it can be hard to remember that on a day-to-day basis.

I have the full range of emotion. I've never been one to have excessive anger—it comes out four times a year and usually involves Christmas decoration storage—but I do have really sad sads and really happy happies. I'm still that way, even though I take medication, but I do try to keep myself on an even-ish keel.

I tell my kids, "You make the decision how you're going to start out your day." I understand not having the energy to get yourself out of bed when you have actual depression. I get that, but I also struggle when I am generally totally fine. I have to decide as soon as I plant my feet on the ground what kind of day I'm going to have. The way I think about it is that you approach everything with a smile and a positive attitude until someone backs into you in the parking lot. Then you recalibrate and figure out what to do.

Sometimes you just feel bad, and you don't necessarily have to do anything about it or make a change. You just have to feel it. I'm trying to teach the kids that too. I'll say, "The fact is, I miss Grandpa Jerry. I'll feel better in a little bit, but right now my body's going to feel better if I cry."

My favorite thing to do to boost my mood is to walk and listen to my favorite music and just let my brain go entirely to mush. But trust me, it can't technically be considered a workout. It's more of a "zone out." It feels like meditation. And now with all the other stuff I do in a day as a mom, I miss doing it as much as I used to.

Realistically, the only time I have to go for a walk at the end of the day is after I've just spent twenty minutes wrestling toddlers into pajamas. Why do they make those holes so small? It's like trying to get an eel into an electrical outlet. I'm sweating and frustrated and tired. And then I'm supposed to exercise?

Kristin wanted to be workout buddies. Can you believe that? I told her I'd go on a hike with her sometime. But then she reminded me that we'd see one snake and it would be game over. Maybe I'd go bowling. That's a workout, right? I do love bowling alley food. You can get any fried thing you want there.

KRISTIN

Bowling is not a workout! Anything where you wear jeans and drink beer when you do it does not an exercise routine make. Jen hates exercising so much that when the apocalypse comes, I'm going to have to cut her loose. She'll bring down the team. Jen's so anti-workout that she thinks I'm a fitness guru. She saw me shoot a basket once and thought I should play for the Lakers.

To me, that's what it all comes down to: If there's a zombie apocalypse, can I survive? You can if you're not too skinny and you're not too fat. You need enough stuff on you to bunker down for a while, but you also need to be fit enough to run if you have to. I'll tell you something right now: I am the person you want around if there are walking dead on the scene. Yeah, I'm not stick thin, but I'm a leader and I'm very, very strong. 'Cause I work out. Three to six times a month.

I do keep trying to get Jen to work out with me. I'll propose, "I will trade you one workout for two conversations about crystals and your kids' dreams," but she never bites (and yet, somehow, I still know a ton about the healing power of agate). She should totally do it because her body responds really quickly to the lightest routine. If she just does something with hand weights, two days later you see a difference. When she got married, she was really careful about what she was eating, she actually did some workouts, and she got so skinny. Maybe too skinny. I let it go because people are le cuckoo when it comes to weddings, but if she had slid any skinnier, I would have staged an intervention. Jen is really lucky—she has a feminine figure, whatever weight she's at. She has a tiny waist, a high butt, and perfectly proportional boobs. I'm built like a tree trunk. All of my weight is in my middle, which means I pretty much look pregnant all the time.

But it's not just about losing weight. I want us to support one another in our fitness goals, and we don't do that. In fact, we do the opposite of that. We've actually watched workout videos together while we drank wine and ate some cheesy bar dip. It's not like we haven't tried. One night during our first tour, we convinced each other we were going to work out after every show. We told ourselves, "We can do this! We will work out every night and get super fit." When we had this discussion we were wearing our Spanx and shoveling three-cheese pizza into our mouths. The next day, we took an Uber to a mall in the middle of nowhere. Jen bought really expensive running shoes, I bought super sporty workout pants, and then we wore the cute shoes and sporty clothes to the nearest Applebee's, where we pounded chicken fingers and ranch dressing. We did not go to the gym on tour. Not. One. Single. Time.

I just need to make my peace with the fact that Jen is not a gym buddy. Sure, she likes to lift spirits (in more ways than one), but that is where lifting ends for her. I grew up a lot sportier than Jen did. I played baseball and volleyball and did cheerleading. And I like feeling physical and strong. It's weird, but it feels like I'm doing something for the family by taking care of myself that way. I'm not by any means a gym rat. In fact, I went to a gym to sign up about a year ago, and you know how they make you sit and talk and listen to their whole sales pitch? The client services guy asked me why I was there, and I told him, "I just want to lose some baby weight." He said, "Oh, yeah? How old is your baby?" and I said, "She's five," and he was like, "That's not baby weight. That's just weight." See ya later, dude.

I don't love going to the gym solo because I don't enjoy the elliptical or the treadmill, but I love taking classes. I take Zumba, barre, spin, you name it. I just took my first boxing class. It felt amazing to hit something. I loved it. But there was one time I took a class I did not have any business being in. It was called Sensual Cardio, which I thought meant it came with a massage afterward. The instructor called out, "Okay, now get in touch with your body and loosen your hips." She started moving her hips so freely and was so sexy. My hips wouldn't move. It looked like I was Hula-Hooping and smelling something bad at the same time. There wasn't a pole or anything, but we were supposed to do things like slap both hands on the floor and then run them up our body. I was so awkward about it. It was at 2:00 p.m., the sexiest time of the day. I pretended I was like a sex-positive superhero who did everything in slow motion, but in the mirror it looked like I was having a seizure. When the instructor asked us to freestyle our sexiest move, I just flipped over onto my back and put my legs up. I don't know what sexy moves those twenty-somethings were doing, but mine involved the least amount of work, so who is the smart one?

So, I like to take (most) classes. I also like to quit classes.

I've taken the first two of a lot of classes—cardio kickboxing, boot camp, CrossFit—and then I got caught up in work or school functions and my enthusiasm died. I don't think any mother should be held to the policy of late fees, cancellation fees, twenty-four-hour notice, whatever. I think you should just get a stamp on your agreement that says "She's got a toddler," and it's like a get-out-of-jail-free card.

I actually got kicked out of a yoga class too, just like Jen! The hot girl next to me tooted, I called her out on it, and the men revolted. I was wearing some sweet XL Farmers National Bank threads, and I had my fat pants on, and they got all "How dare you? Pick on somebody your own size."

Every time I work out, I know I will feel better about myself when I'm done, but I will do *everything else* first, just so I don't have to go to the gym. *Gotta catch up on software updates / get a new passport photo / organize the junk drawer!*

I'm in this weird place where I recognize there are people with real weight issues and that fifteen pounds doesn't qualify as a huge deal for most people, but fifteen pounds feels big to me. It's so hard to crack through (I have been the exact same weight for four years). Also, I'm not sure that I completely wanna do what I have to do to get rid of the extra weight. I did CrossFit and Whole30 at the same time when I was really trying to get trim. And I lost six pounds. I was working out five days a week, and I was eating such a restricted diet. And I'll tell you something: I'd do a workout, and then I was wrecked for the rest of the day. I missed work and I had to sleep during the day because I was so exhausted. I couldn't keep it up.

So it's a balance for me. I know that if I am persistently concerned about how I look, like being frustrated with my weight, I have to get myself thinking about something else or I just spiral. I'm descending a set of stairs until it becomes not about what I look like but about who I am and how I am no good. Then pretty soon, it's hard to get back up those stairs again.

Working out, making good food choices, saying no to wine can be really tough. It can feel like we never get a break, so when we do, it feels like we've earned it. We have *earned* a dessert or a second glass of wine or a lazy night on the sofa. That's important every now and then, but after a while we all have our own internal mechanism that says, "Okay, lady, you gotta get off your ass and get moving." And what I can tell you from having eighty pounds of baby weight after Eleanor is that it super sucks to take the first steps at any point. It's painful and slow. I had fat in weird places moving around so much that my back boobs needed a sports bra just as much as my front ones. But just doing a little bit helps push the pedal in a way that our mom brains desperately need. We have to pump healthy blood through our mom bods. By no means am I a fitness guru—I struggle just like everyone else—but one thing I do that helps is to think to myself when I work out, *Hell yes! I am here. I am strong. I am a mom.* It's so dorky but it helps me feel empowered, and I need every boost or visual I can muster sometimes.

I've had bouts of depression, and I've also wrestled with ADHD. I have more of a love-hate relationship with meds than Jen does. Every time I talk to my psychiatrist and she suggests, "Let's try this," I bawl. I worry that I won't be myself anymore if I am on meds. It might be because when my ADHD got diagnosed, they put me on one of the earliest forms of Ritalin, and it was so strong that it made me virtually catatonic. Some part of my brain must have been thinking, *Hey, people seem to prefer this weird zombie-like version of you.* It made me resent medication, and it made me feel very ashamed and weak and broken. I don't think that way about other people, but for some reason I can't always grant myself that same grace. I ask myself, *What's wrong with you? Why can't you just get out of this funk? You've got everything, and you're still a mess*, and that just layers the guilt on top of everything else. I like talking about it with Jen because she'll ask me, "Well, are you going to tell somebody who needs glasses that their eyes are a failure, or are you going to help them pick out frames?" Or sometimes she'll just say, "Knock that shit off now." And it helps.

Jen likes to say that my brain's more efficient than hers, like I have four screens going and she has one. She keeps playing the exact same episode of *House Hunters International* again and again all day long while I toggle between four stations. Our brains work very differently—differently from each other's and differently from everybody else's. Yours does too. We're a testament to the fact that your brain doesn't have to be perfect to do what you need it to do and to bring your own specific and interesting thing to the world. And we're a testament to the fact that your life doesn't have to be perfect for it to be what you want. You'll never feel 100 percent ready to do anything, but just do it anyway.

I want my kids to think that too, so I try to be as honest as I can with them. I think it's a little bit on us to lay the groundwork for being more candid and real. Besides, your kids notice when you're pretending, especially as they get older and you start to talk to them differently. The sooner we show them we're human, the faster they will learn empathy and compassion.

These days, when my kids are being really rough, I just tell them, "You know what? I'm literally doing the best job I can, and I am near tears. I am losing it. Do you want to help me be a better mommy? Just give me a break."

They look at me like *Oh, shit. She's about to crack.* To me, being honest with the kids is more important than being perfect for the kids. They can sniff out phoniness, so I give it to them straight at a real honest level. And they give it right back. If I'm putting up a sunshine and happiness front because we're meeting up with new friends, they'll say, "Mommy was crying in the car before we got here." It's just healthier to be on the up-and-up.

I thought about this one day when I posted this super cute picture of Eleanor before her dance recital. If you were scrolling through Instagram and saw her gorgeous smiling face, you'd think, *Damn, that family has it together.* But what you wouldn't have seen was the fact that we almost missed the recital because I had completely forgotten about it until an hour beforehand. The whole lead-up to that photo was a crying, screaming, scrambling mess. It just so happened that it took place the same week that Kate Spade and Anthony Bourdain took their own lives, and it made me think about how we're not doing one another any favors by pretending that things are always rainbows and unicorns. I made sure to caption the photo to let everyone know that it wasn't telling the whole story. That's really the thing, isn't it? We never know the whole story. I don't want anybody to feel like she can't say when things are going awesome, but sometimes they're not awesome. Let's just give one another license to say, "Yeah, I'm in hell." And then let's let one another know we're not alone there. Belly up to the bar. I'll buy you a drink.

I GET DARK
SO HARD

For all our complaints about the difficulties of being a
parent, at our core we are mostly wildly and absurdly aware
of how manageable most of our gripes are. Yeah, it sucks to be
tired all the time and to spend countless hours cooking meals
that line the garbage can ten minutes after they're on the table,
but you get through those things with enough laughter, perspective, and prosecco. There are some things, though, that
run deeper, the things that actually keep you up at night when
you're pretending—even to yourself—that you're just worried about whether everyone thought you were the fun girl at
that party last week or whether you were the girl everybody
made fun of after that party last week. We're not talking about
garden-variety gal-in-peril because of an aggro alien/lunatic/
tsunami horror. No. It's the idea of your kid getting sick or
being in danger, or the fear that you're failing so bad as a mom

that you're ruining him for life—that's what will really mess you up and haunt your dreams.

KRISTIN

*Everybody has their fears. Mine are doctors and magi-*cians. One makes things disappear, and the other reads a scan and tells you something has appeared. Either way, they freak me out. Doctors scare me so hard that I have never had a mammogram. The whole idea terrifies me. Lab coats, tests, the words "dense tissue"—all of it. I hate the medical experience. (Although, if someone offered me a free tummy tuck, I'd be on the table tomorrow.) I've got absolutely zero love for magicians, which might not make sense to you immediately, but they do that thing where they make you look at one hand while they do weird stuff with the other hand, and I don't trust them. They give me nightmares. The only reason I like doctors is because their antianxiety medication is magical.

Nightmares are scary because they feel real, and they just get realer as you get older and the stakes get higher. You go from being scared that people will laugh because you still sleep with a stuffed animal, to being scared that no one will sleep with you at all, to then being scared that your baby will die in her sleep. Yeah, when you become a mom, nightmares get real.

As a kid, my biggest nightmare was Freddy Krueger. I mean, he was a creepy burnt man who haunts dreams. Hello, insomnia. My friends and I used to scare the crap out of ourselves, chanting, "One, two, Freddy's coming for you. Three, four, better lock your door. Five, six, grab your crucifix. Seven, eight, gonna stay up late. Nine, ten, Freddy's back again." A few rounds of that and I was ready to jump into bed with my parents, something I continued doing way beyond when it was age appropriate. I'd take off my bra and be like, "What are we watching tonight, guys? *Night Court*, then *Carson*?"

My daughter's Freddy Krueger is Ursula from *The Little Mermaid*. Yes, the Disney movie with the ginger mermaid and the spunky singing crab. Ursula is the reason Colin and I had a third bunkmate for three weeks last summer. If Eleanor even hears her name, I guarantee she's not sleeping in her bed that night. If she sees anything that *reminds* her of Ursula, it's game over. You guys, we live in Southern California. Beach scenes are very popular. Also, my son's name is Finn. Whenever we watch *The Little Mermaid*, Eleanor sits on my lap, and when Ursula appears I can feel Eleanor's butt cheeks clench on my legs. She does not let go until that woman-octopus is off the screen.

Our fears are so irrational. There's no explaining them, but it's crazy how we can't just push them aside and tell ourselves, *Eh, no such thing as an ashy blade-fingered murder man or a mean octopus lady coming to take me to the netherworld. Carry on.* Even when we totally understand the facts, our minds skip merrily around them and remain focused on the illogical threat. It's like we don't even want to get rid of those fears sometimes. In fact, it's the total opposite. We want to get all up in our fears' faces, so close that we can see their crow's-feet and clogged pores. Even when I was younger, I'd poke my fears with a stick. We'd have a sleepover and someone would bust out a Ouija board. *Let's order pizza, paint our nails, AND OPEN*

A PORTAL INTO HELL. You'd never ask a Ouija board, "Hey, is my Aunt Marge there? She had a wonderful lasagna recipe, and I have a couple of questions." No way. We'd always say something like, "If someone is going to die tonight, give us a sign."

Why do we put ourselves through this? I have a theory. Getting all close up with the scary stuff is like a dry run in case something really bad happens in our life.

When I was eleven, my cousin Kurt told me that if I looked into a mirror and said "Bloody Mary" three times, a witch would appear in my reflection and cut my head off. So of course I went right home and did it. *Bloody Mary, Bloody Mary, Bloody Mary.* Then *boom*! I instantly dropped to the floor and hid under my dresser so long that I peed my pants to avoid getting decapitated on the way to the bathroom. When my mom found the pee spot she bit my head off, so my fears weren't entirely unfounded.

Maybe we think that if we really understand our fear, if we invite it in for a nice meal, get to know its quirks, make a few disarming jokes, we can stop it from piercing our rib cage and plucking our heart out with a spoon.

I use this kind of reverse voodoo all the time as a parent. I call it the "mom tremors." I will think the worst possible thing about my kids, about something horrible happening to them. *Okay, I'm going to imagine that my son gets hit by a car. What would that be like?* I'll imagine the car screeching and *ughhhhh-hhhhhh.* I mean, that is the most torturing thought, but it's like I have to think it to keep it from actually coming true. When I'm freaking out, those images are really in there, and they run on a loop. I will literally tell myself, *Kristin, cool it*. I have found that I have to actively participate in getting my brain out of that space or I will stay there, feeling terrified.

I think all moms do this, right? We feel like we're going to be able to preempt this bad thing because we thought it through so there's no way it will actually take place. Not that we take any actual steps to protect ourselves. It's more like we're telling the universe, *No need to hit* PLAY *on that scenario 'cause we've already got it covered via the world's most excruciatingly real virtual reality device: mom mind.*

Someone once told me that to worry is to suffer twice—and, man, do I wish I could just suffer once. So I try to keep myself from stepping in the sadness quicksand, which means sometimes I get on YouTube and watch old Bob Newhart episodes. You've got to get something else going in your brain to distract yourself so that you're not missing out on life while you're worrying about something that *might* happen. I go with old man comedy.

Sometimes it works. Sometimes it doesn't. You never know what's going to set you off. Even my kids scare the crap out of me sometimes. They say the creepiest shit. They have said the following to me:

Mommy, I want to wear your eyes.

When you drown, does blood pour out of your face?

Sometimes when I'm alone I talk to her. Her. That one right there.

What the hell, you two? I can't escape. Even when I'm asleep.

If nightmares were like beers, these would be my nightmare lites (my Nighty Lite): I have these dreams where I left my kids somewhere and I can't get to them. I left them at Target, or I left them in the middle of a grocery store, and my phone won't work. I can't get *any* technology to work, and there is no help. I'm thinking, *I'll get you, I'll get you—just hold on*, but I can't make my fingers work on my phone.

And now, I have the Guinness, the dark heavy beer of nightmares, the one that I have a hard time talking about, that literally shakes me to the core. I have this repetitive nightmare that I only imagined my children. *They never really existed.* I wake up and Finn and Eleanor were just a dream, a figment of my imagination. It's like an episode of *Black Mirror* targeted directly at me.

And then I wake up and someone is asking me to make scrambled eggs.

What is my subconscious doing to me?

As every one of you moms know, the biggest fear is that something is going to happen to your children. Everybody has had those terrible dark moments with your kids that are crippling. You pull them back to the curb just in time. Or you almost let them eat something without checking the label for allergy info.

Losing a child is absolutely unfathomable, except I fathom. Good lord, do I fathom. Now that I have these two people in my life, I know exactly the size and shape of the loss if anything were to happen to them, and it is f*cking enormous. My son gives me "no reason hugs," and my daughter will crawl in next to me so tight we look like human Legos. There is no single part of me that can live without that.

The flip side of worrying is that it makes you hyperaware of what you're scared to lose. I've been really freaking lucky in my life. Think about those parents who have lost kids, or friends who are dealing with kids who have real difficulties or challenges. We've had so many moms reach out to us on #IMOMSOHARD who are themselves sick, or whose kids are sick, or who have gone through infant loss or toddler loss or child loss. We've gotten the most incredible, brave comments from all these wonderful mothers. I don't know where they put it, that kind of sadness, but damn if they're not the strongest people we've ever met. Some of them take the time to write in and say, "Thank you for making us laugh." We always have the same reaction when we read those messages. These incredible women are suffering unimaginable pain, but their instinct is to reach out and express kindness and gratitude. That's why we are amazed by how women are extraordinary—they are capable of giving even when so much has been taken from them.

That's the emotional reality of motherhood. You're like a boxer, taking blow after blow to the chin and then having to stand up again. Your heart takes a beating, going from pain to love to laughter to heartache to joy. You can have every one of those emotions within fifteen minutes.

There are times when my head gets in a place where I can't even enjoy the nice moments. We'll be running through the sprinklers, covered in grass cuttings and Fanta, and I get this feeling like things are too good right now. I'm constantly waiting for a shoe to drop. I had to take all these tests recently because we are estate planning, and I braced myself: *Well, here it comes. This is where I find out I have Parkinson's.*

Which brings me to the other big fear: dying and leaving your kids behind. I have to give it to my mom. She has absolutely everything planned for her death—what lifesaving measures she wants taken, who gets her jewelry, what songs to play at her funeral, which neighborhood of heaven she'd prefer. When we were kids, she would tear up before every weekend getaway with my dad and say, "Kids, in case our plane explodes in a fiery inferno, the instructions for my funeral are in the death drawer. Love you." Personally, I hope the afterlife is like the last scene of *Titanic* where Jack is standing at the bottom of the stairs looking at the festivities. I'll say goodbye to life on earth and then find myself looking in through the window of my favorite pub, my husband, friends, and family hooting and drinking and telling tales, hoping I'll be allowed in to stay forever.

While we were in the thick of our end-of-life planning, I told Colin, "If I die before you, you've got to get remarried." He laughed. "I'm not ever getting remarried." And I said, "Oh, no. You will not turn my home into a frat house. You have to get remarried pretty quickly after I die because *you will* die without someone to help you, and then our kids will be orphans."

Women are practical. Before we're gone, we're already drafting the dating profile: "My husband needs to find a partner immediately because without me he'll yell at the kids too much and no one will ever go to school with clean clothes." That's what we're thinking. How do we provide a wonderful, warm, loving, supportive environment for our children? Our husbands, on the other hand, are thinking, *If I'm dead, so is your sex life.*

Colin likes to explain to me in vivid detail—smiling and laughing but not fully joking—that if *he* dies and I eventually remarry, he will hover over our bed like the ghost of Christmas past and bugger my new husband while he's humping me. That's my husband's main concern: that someone else will have sex with me. *What?! That's your big concern? Not the heartache I'd face or the well-being of our children? You'll be dead and gone, our children will be fatherless, but you're concerned about me nailing another dude when you're six feet under?*

My new end-of-life plan is to outlive Colin.

JEN

My husband and I have also been estate planning. I'm scared to death that I'm going to forget to find somebody who will clean the kids' ears for them, trim their fingernails, and match outfits together when they put the laundry away, because my husband, well, that's not his strong suit. I don't want my kids going to school and having everybody think they're color-blind or they don't know the difference between pajama bottoms and a leotard. That kind of stuff scares me. I don't want their lives to be harder than they absolutely have to be if I die. My parents divorced, so I know how hard it is to not have both parents around. All you want is time with them.

As part of our estate planning, we had to designate who will take care of the kids if, God forbid, we both fall off a cliff (yet another reason not to go hiking). I feel bad that it's not Kristin. We have my sister-in-law raising them, and we put my brother in charge of legal and money (he doesn't really like hugs but he does have an MBA). My sister-in-law is real gentle and has raised one of her own, and he's a smart kid. Odds are, she's a much better parent than we are. But I know that it doesn't matter because Kristin's going to be on their ass for the rest of their damn lives. And I would do the same for Eleanor and Finn. They're like my adopted kids. If Kristin goes, I'm going to make sure Colin's new wife remembers all their show-and-tell days, talent shows, and all that kind of stuff.

I told Brit, "You have to start dating immediately after I die. You have to get remarried," kind of expecting him to say something about how he would be too sad about losing me to think about dating for a long time. Instead, he said, "Oh, I've already picked the woman. She's married, but . . ." Whoa, whoa, whoa, mister. I said "immediately *after I die.*"

But I'm glad he's thinking about it (just not too much or in too much detail). I want him to find somebody who will be nice to him and nice to our kids, who will love them as I do. And then Brit said, "Oh, and if I die, don't you dare get a hot dude to share your bed. Don't you dare." Honey, based on what you know about me, how great a priority do you think sex is going to be? Sex is not what I'm going to be looking for. I'm for sure going to find a gay man to be my companion and go antique shopping with me and listen to my ghost stories.

I care about Brit's life after I go, but of course I'm most worried about how my death would affect the kids. My husband's mom passed away twenty years ago now, and he was devastated by it. I can see how the sadness affects him even now. I know he wishes she had met our kids. He talks about what she would've

sung to them and how she would've delighted in their unique-
ness. I never met Bobbye Lou, but in some weird way I miss her
too. I think we would have been fast friends. She studied musical theater and liked sewing and adored her family. When my
son was born, I asked her to send me a sign when she was near
him, and as I rocked him, I kept thinking of owls. Now whenever I see an owl, I tell the kids that their Grandma Bobbye is
thinking about them and loving them.

When Dash was young and learning about his family, I told
him about his grandparents, including Brit's mother, of course. It's
not like she didn't exist. So I said, "You have Mimi, Kiki, Grandma
Barbara, and Grandpa Jerry, and there's also Grandma Bobbye.
She's one of your angels, and if you ever wanna tell her you love
her or say hi before you go to bed, just say it up to the sky." After I
told him that, Dash started to say on occasion, "Oh, I was talking
to Grandma Bobbye." We'll ask, "You were? Where did you see
her?" and he'll point up to the ceiling. Totally not creepy.

So when my dad died this year, we told Dash that now
Grandpa Jerry is one of his angels too. My dad's dying was
the hardest thing I've ever had to deal with. I didn't want the
world to just keep going, and yet it did. Relentlessly. Traffic
jams, commercials, birthday parties, the need to eat and sleep
and take care of two kids who also needed to eat and sleep—it
all kept going as if my heart hadn't imploded. It sucked. All I
wanted to do was sit around and be sad about losing my dad.
It's so hard to be a mom and a human and a friend when you're
grieving, because the death is all you're thinking about.

We were friends. He knew the coolest bar in every city. He
knew about music and culture and art. He said I could be whatever

I wanted to be, but he really hoped I'd be an attorney. He went to Taco Bell so much. My dad thought so hard about how to live your life, how to be your own true self—and he was very much that himself. I want to honor him by being that way too. I want to pass that on, to help people know how to get good with who they are.

I'll tell you when you really start to feel like an adult. It's not when you have a kid; it's when you lose a parent. And kids themselves are no help. We'll be having a perfectly happy day, and my son, who is learning his numbers, will ask, "How old was Grandpa Jerry when he died, seventy-nine or eighty-eight?" And I'm thinking, *Why is this your story problem? Can't you just figure out when the trains are going to collide like everyone else? Can you lay off the Grandpa Jerry thing, kid?* I was fine for like thirty minutes, and now I'm freshly sad again.

I cry my head off a lot, but it's not out of weakness. While I'm crying, I will tear your arms off and beat you to death with them. It's just how I get rid of this bad feeling.

I'm gradually getting into a numb phase, which I'm sort of happy to be in. I had been crying four times a day, and then it dwindled down, and now I'm like a little distanced from things. It's operational. I'm a functional griever at the moment. Normally, I'm pretty in touch with what I'm feeling, but I feel somewhat detached right now. But the flip side of something terrible happening is that you realize very acutely what makes you happy. I'm complaining less. With stuff that might usually bother me, I'm taking a new attitude: *Whatever. Tell me when it's a big deal.*

I'm not completely numb, of course. I get those "mom tremors" Kristin was talking about, and I do feel some things—like anxiety. Sometimes, life as a parent is one big panic attack. There is so much to worry about. Everything on a development calendar sends me into hysterics. I'm convinced my daughter will never read. I worry about dirty needles at the beach. Broken glass at the beach. Fish hooks at the beach. I worry about whether the car seat chest bar is *directly* over the nipple area or that my sleeping child in the back seat has actually broken her neck and that's why her head is at that inhuman angle. Other things I worry about: Things falling from the sky. Red dye #5. That my kid is going to be the "dandruffy" kid. Bone density. Kids getting their teeth knocked out. That they'll hate me for, like, extended periods of time. Or worse, that they'll think we're buddies.

I try to take it day by day. Look, I've read mountains of self-help books and know what I should be doing. I need to focus on the big stuff, like what kinds of people my kids are going to turn into. Will they wipe their boogers in library books? Or will they let littler kids go in front of them at Disneyland? Most of the time, and this is on them, not me, they will. (Both the Disneyland and the boogers.)

Some parents' ultimate goal is to be able to say things like "The only thing I can get my kid to read is *Architectural Digest*," or "She's *obsessed* with dodecahedrons." But that's not what I want, unless it's what they want. We have email addresses for the kids where I send photos or notes from the heart. Before I get on a plane, I send them a picture, a love note, or whatever. The message I'm trying to get across is that I want them to be kind, hardworking, and funny, in that order.

I don't care if they're a doctor, molecular scientist, senator, law professor, Rhodes scholar, bioengineer, philanthropist, Supreme

Court justice. I don't even really care if they know what those things are. I tell them, "Mommy's going to love you no matter what kind of surgeon you become."

As long as they're kind and they work hard, they'll probably be okay in life, and if they're funny they can deal with whatever gets thrown at them, you know? I hope they know I love them, that I want only the best for them in life, and that even when I'm gone, they'll carry the good stuff in their hearts. (And the secret stuff in the small zippered pocket of their handbags. Maybe not my son, but again, whatever they want.)

Most nights before Dash goes to bed, I tell him, "Do you know what my happiest day ever was? The day you were born." And he goes, "That's my happiest day too." It's pretty hard to feel numb when you hear that.

I LIVE
AND LET LIVE
SO HARD

In our videos and live shows, we tend to steer away from politics. We have thoughts and views, of course, because we are a couple of strong, opinionated broads (just ask our husbands), but we're careful because we don't want to be divisive. And the reason we don't want to be divisive is because we want to re-mind everybody who comes to the #IMOMSOHARD party that no matter what your thoughts and views are, if your six-year-old is being a jerk in the Olive Garden, we'll let you borrow our tablet to calm him down. We're also going to give you a look that says, *Girl, I've been there*, and then send a bottle of Chianti to your table.

Being a mom is a great equalizer. We all love our kids, and we all have to clean up their barf at 2:00 a.m. If you're a mom and you watch our videos or come to our shows or read this book because you had the worst, shittiest day, we want to make you feel just the tiniest bit less awful and less alone, whether you're wearing a burka or booty shorts, because we are a few billion strong.

These are our politics: We care about our kids. We care about your kids. We care about you. So if we can help you, if we can take care of you, we will. That's what's going to save the world. It's not going to be a bunch of dudes fighting it out. No, it's going to be a bunch of moms whose superpower is love.

KRISTIN

Every time we leave the house, my kids take it as an invita-tion to drop some truth in their outside voices. "Hey, how come the guy sitting next to us doesn't have any legs?" Or my daughter will say, "What if I'm on my bed and my stuffed animal puts its hand on my vagina?" (We just had a conversation about stranger danger, so there are a lot of "what if" scenarios coming at us.) We want our kids to be tuned in to the world and its wonders, but sometimes, we put that business on lockdown.

Colin and I have been working with the kids on what's okay to say and what should stay private—and most of the time, we laugh it off when they step in it. No harm done. But there are two things that really set us off that we have placed on the Does Not Fly list.

The first thing we tell our kids is that you don't get to comment on how much money people have or don't have. Right now, we talk about money, because those are easy to understand terms. What we want the conversation to evolve into is taking a beat before you judge someone, because you don't know their whole story. Now, this is hard because we live in Los Angeles. You drive around town and see little houses and then giant houses. There are get-along cars, and then there are fancy cars, etc. So Finn has started to use the words "rich" and "poor." He'll say, "Whoa, they must be rich!" when he sees a house that has one of those gates that you open with some kind of electronic device, or "Oh, he must be poor" when he sees someone who's down on their luck hustling on the corner for money. My husband and I just come undone when we hear that. We try to instill in them that there are people in the world who are suffering and there are people in the world who need help. When you see someone who doesn't have what they need, your heart should feel something. I want my kids to know that just because someone's homeless doesn't mean their shit stinks any worse. Shit is shit. So when our kids talk about how much someone has or doesn't have, we're like, *Slow your roll, buddy*. You don't know what the scenario is. You don't know what their overhead is. That person over there could be house poor, and that person over there could have a lot in the bank because they choose to live a more pragmatic lifestyle. You don't know. That person could be upside-down on their loan. As soon as you can, you're going to read *The Millionaire Next Door*, and you're going to understand what rich and poor really are. You're going to think about things like how much that guy has to work every day to afford that house. Does he get to see his family? Does he come home at 5:05 and spend time with his kids? What about the mom? Does she have to work a double shift and double-coupon to pay for private school? We tell them that when you see somebody who has something, you have to assume the best—that they've worked hard for it. And if they don't have as much as you do, they're probably working really hard to make it so they're comfortable.

When I say stuff like that, Finn will say, "What? I was just saying that Eli's family has a big house." I'll say, "Finn, I like where your head is at, kid, because real estate is a smart long-term investment, but they don't have much of a yard, and building another story on top is a nightmare architecturally, plus being outside is important." He'll reply, "Mom, I don't know what you're saying." I don't know when to let go.

Sometimes I think he might be getting the message. Our neighbors in our old neighborhood had two campers in their driveway. They were a divorced couple, their daughter was pretty sick, and nobody had a ton of money, so Mom was living in one of the RVs while they shared the responsibility of caring for their kid. So these were "filling a basic human need for shelter" RVs, not "Hey, I'm retired and road-tripping to Florida" RVs. The neighbors were just doing what they had to do to get by. It couldn't have been easy 'cause most of the neighborhood had more of a suburban vibe. Finn took one look at that driveway after one of our talks about not making assumptions, and he was like, "Boy, our neighbors must work really hard because they have *two* campers." That's my boy.

The second rule we have in our home is you don't get to comment on how people look. Period. The thing is, my kids still can't reliably distinguish between positive and negative, so the de facto rule is *just don't*. Blanket statement. Don't say anything. Don't comment on how people look. That guy does not want to be referred to as a pirate just because he has one leg and you think that's awesome. If somebody looks different than you and you find yourself staring, you have to smile at them. If you're looking at them because they're in a wheelchair or they have a purple Mohawk, you can't look at them like they're scary. You have to smile. You need to make it a little bit friendlier. Your curiosity is great, it's natural—we applaud it!—but it should not make other people feel bad. So *do not say anything*. You don't know how to do it yet. We'll let you look, but it has to be with a kind face.

Even when you have a lot of life under your belt, this stuff is tricky. If my dad's in a conversation and he finds you boring or just doesn't get where you're coming from, he shuts it down. He's like me, and he doesn't have the wherewithal or the desire to suffer fools. He doesn't filter. He just says, "Gotta go," and he'll walk away. But if he's on board with you, he'll love you for the rest of his life. My dad says how he feels, and he says it with vigor. Countless times, he has looked at Jen and me and said, "I'm so goddamn proud of you two dizzy broads. You girls are so bright and *funny*!" And it fills our bucket. Once you are in the inner circle with Dewey, you are in it for life. He doesn't even care if the result isn't great. For instance, when I was fifteen I broke up with a guy I was dating. Big whoop. But my dad still asks me about the guy, and I have to say, "Dad, I don't know what Cole Bradley is doing these days." And he'll continue, "That was a nice kid, Cole Bradley, back in the summer when you and Lynn used to . . ." And I'll be like, "Uuugghhhh,

Dad. I literally couldn't pick him out in a lineup. I have no idea." And my dad will quietly mutter, "I liked that kid."

I always get a little nervous when my dad meets someone who's different from him. I'm on alert for him, waiting for him to say something that is going to require some 'splaining from me. He's driving for Uber now, and a week or so ago he was telling me, "Kristin, I drove a fella the other day. Ya know, he was one of them gays. The gays love me. They see me as a great DIY makeover project. They take one look and they think, *Now* there's *a good flip*." My dad continued, revving up with louder volume, "I don't give two shits about what they do in the bedroom. That's their business." I clenched my stomach, held my breath, and waited for my dad to finish his sentence, and then he said, "And dammit if it wasn't a blast driving that guy around. We had a gas! His name was Gerard, and he smelled like a million bucks. I couldn't keep my eyes on the road because he was just dressed so spiffy." Five stars for you, Dad!

My mom fantasy is that my kids will grow into adults who will defend the weak and, if given the opportunity, will lead with humility and kindness. What that means in plain English is that I want my kids to defend the kid who wants to be a professional Hula-Hooper or the girl who wants to dress like Indiana Jones. I want them to be compassionate to the loner. This world is a big place, and we all feel like square pegs from time to time. It's just nice to think that maybe in the years to come our kids will help make that world a bit happier, a bit nicer, and a bit easier. I would also like them to stop wiping their flippin' toothpaste on my bath towel, but that's probably asking for too much.

JEN

I went through a lot of changes after I had kids. Like, when I drive now, it's with my hands at 10:00 and 2:00 on the steering wheel, I obey all posted signs, and I check my blind spots. Before kids, I multitasked while driving—eating a sandwich, chatting on the phone, scream-singing to music with the radio all the way up. Pre-kids, we used to go out to dinner at 8:00. Now we eat at 5:00 at home. I had money, but now I'm broke. I used to do nightly online shopping for shoes, and now I search "Best value SUV with a third row" or "How much DHA is enough?" But one of the biggest changes I noticed was that after I became a mom, I saw everybody as someone else's child.

The little cretin who took my daughter's Munchkin? Someone's kid. The lady screwing up my lampshade return at T.J. Maxx? Someone's kid. The boy who peed in my planter? Someone's kid (ahem, Kristin's, ahem). It's not like I didn't know this before. I'm no biologist, but I got how the whole parent-child thing worked. But becoming a mother myself just made me way more aware that everybody is just a tiny person at heart, trying their best. And we all have our shit, you know? Like maybe that asshole wanted to give some poofs to his sister because she spilled hers. Or maybe the T.J. Maxx lady just found out her niece has cancer and was distracted. Or maybe Finn's mom never taught him what a toilet looks like.

So it turns me inside out, you guys, seeing someone have an extra hard time of it because of who they are. Life is freaking tough enough without getting shit on by other people, or worse, knowing your kid is getting shit on. It kills knowing that somewhere out there there is a mom whose heart is being crushed like a grape. I believe people are born who they are. The things that make them different aren't moral failings or weaknesses or mistakes. I've been trying to teach my kids this from day one. I don't want my kids' lives to be hard. And as much as I don't want other people making their lives harder, I desperately don't want them to be the dick making other people's lives harder.

Here's what my philosophy is: if you aren't hurting a kid or a dog, I don't give a damn what you do. And frankly, I wish other people would get on board.

My son had a thing at school recently that really got to me. We had to get the kids thermoses for their lunches, so we went to Costco and bought a bright pink one for Delilah and a monster one for Dash, which he loved. But it turned out that at school Dash sits by a girl who told him she didn't like his thermos because she doesn't like monsters because they're scary. So, while I was out of town, he came home and told his dad, "Rosie doesn't like my monster thermos. Can I get a new one?" I melted into a puddle when I heard that. Way to look out for a sista, little man. And Brit decided to just switch thermoses. Delilah loves the monster thermos. Dash likes pink. Problem solved.

So Dash brought the pink one to school, and the teacher told him he couldn't bring a girls' thermos to school. When my husband told me about it, I went dead quiet. My mouth could not catch up to my brain. In California? In the twenty-first century? It's a damn thermos. It keeps hot stuff hot and cold stuff cold. Where is the threat in that? It wasn't about to explode shrapnel. Or even glitter. What if that was the only thermos we could afford? What if Dash just loves pink? Kanye West does! Okay, he also went on TV dressed like a Perrier bottle. But still. What if I got a great deal on those thermoses and bought eight? (Very likely scenario.) I said to him, "Here is what you do: you go to the school and you tell them . . ." And then I said some stuff that I don't want to print here.

It reminded me of the time I'd heard about a dad whose son wanted to be a witch for Halloween and his teacher suggested he be a witch on the inside and a doctor on the outside. How messed up is that? Telling your kid to hide who they want to be behind a totally different and way less awesome thing? I hope that kid went as a witch doctor, turned the teacher into a turd, and then made the teacher well again.

My bottom line is that no matter what my kids are, who they are, how they are, whatever they choose to be, I want them to be strong enough to deal with it when eyebrows get raised or grief is given. What I'm teaching them is that if someone gives you grief about who you are, it's their problem, not your problem. Ef them, politely.

Even that thermos experience was a lesson in understanding for me. I try to see the good in people, even if they're hiding it. Who knows what happened in that teacher's life to make her say those things? Maybe she was a bit of a tomboy as a kid and her friends teased her because she wanted to play He-Man instead of She-Ra. Maybe that left a mark that she doesn't want to replicate.

My grandpa had this way about him of asking people questions when he didn't understand them. He was an honestly inquisitive listener. The guy had so many friends, and they were every type of person you can imagine. I used to think he was in the mob because he had a hookup for everything. Nope. He just was cool. And my grandma—talk about a badass strong woman. She had a hair salon in Nebraska before there were even paved streets in town. She told me one time, "I used to do everybody's hair in town. Well, not everybody's. Some people wouldn't come to me because I also did black people's hair." I told her how cool I thought she was for being so brave for the time. She replied very practically, as though I were an idiot, "Jenny, they were just people who needed their hair done. Why would I say no?" Yep.

It's a magical thing about being a mom. The fact that you understand what it's like to live for another person, to love someone so completely, means that you get other moms at a basic level. You can have absolutely fundamentally different views from someone who is also a mother. But we're all just trying to do right by our kids and your kids. If you point a gun at a mom who's standing next to my child and you say, "There's one bullet. I either shoot you or the kid," that mom won't hesitate for a second. She's gonna say, "Me." It doesn't matter who they are or where they pray or if they pray at all. She'll be like, "I volunteer as tribute," every time. Regardless of who you are or what you think or who you screw. Every freaking time.

I feel such a base-level connection to other moms—and it goes beyond the stuff you choose to do with your time and how you approach life. I'm not into that reverse snobbery where I assume someone can't be my friend because they seem to have it more together than I do.

We have tons of friends who could teach a class on being awesome in the mom space. They get professional photographs done of their kids. They have schedules. They eat three meals a day that all contain protein. When they make something from Pinterest, it looks exactly like Pinterest.

For example, Kristin and I have this friend Eileen who is a super hippie, earth mother type. She does yoga—by herself and with her daughters. I think she delivered all her babies by herself in a barn. Her family has chickens, and she collects their eggs, makes omelets, and whips up biscuits with lavender honey. *Everything* she has is homemade. God love her, she probably even crocheted one of those chunky woven blankets that are cluttering up your Facebook feed. Her kids wear crowns of daisies as they frolic through the prairie in hand-sewn frocks. You get the picture.

But if she brings her kids to our house, they're getting Cheetos.

And you know what? If this were a sitcom, we'd play moms who hate her, who resent the hell out of her adorable fluffy chickens and the omega-3s they provide. But the thing is, we don't hate her. She's lovely. Her kids know how to compost, but her family is still totally down to party. I apologized once for having only pizza at a birthday thing. She said, "Oh yeah, we're vegan, but when we're at parties we eat pizza. Lots of it."

It's one of those keep-your-eyes-on-your-own-work sorts of scenarios. Nothing good comes of comparing, and you probably don't have time to criticize anybody else anyway. That time you spent criticizing could probably have been spent trimming your nails or cleaning out somebody's ears.

We know that "mommy wars" sort of exist, but we always wonder if we weren't invited to the party or something. I just feel like we have cool chicks around us. It's been our experience—and we are not unicorns—that moms are awesome. It's not a rose-colored glasses thing—I'm very real about people's shortcomings—but moms are good people. *Women* are good people. One of the best parts of what we do with #IMOMSOHARD is that we get to see on a daily basis in our comment sections and our audiences that people are good, generally speaking.

If there's a mom out there who is the Hall to your Oates and you find out she's sick or she's got a sick kid, you'll bring over a casserole. You may not talk to her while you're there, or you might drop it off and say, "It's a baked ziti. I literally hate everything you think. Warm that up at 350 for twenty minutes, and screw you. There's pine nuts in it, you wench. Don't give it to Jeremy. He's got a food allergy. I respect that, but I despise everything you stand for. I'm pissed off, and I'm gonna put it on your damn front porch. Let me know if you need anything else."

Those are the values we are talking about at work. What I want at the end of the day is what happened when my dad was sick. I was how many thousands of miles away? And chicks I hadn't spoken to in years—ones I disagree with about nearly everything, from who you have a right to marry to whether a football jersey is appropriate church attire—reached out. They said, "Can I go to the grocery store for him?" Not just one woman. It was fifteen of them at least. Kristin's mom lives an hour and a half away from my dad's home, and she told me, "Jen, I went over to your dad's. I gave him a bath. He had some drywall work that needed to be done, and I called a couple of guys and they did that." Can we have more of that, please? My hand to God, that's what saves the universe. Because at the end of the day, regardless of your background or beliefs, we're all somebody's kid.

Yes, I've had wine. Someone high-five me or give me an "amen" please.

A FINAL WORD

It's that time . . . we have to go back to yelling at our kids to get their backpacks on or finish their homework, asking them to pee in the potty, and screaming at them to please not eat the fruit snacks that are stuck to the floor of the minivan.

So, this is the end, ladies. Actually, it's just the beginning, because every day is a new adventure for a mom. Let us leave you with these words of advice: Never whisper into the wind, "What else could possibly go wrong?" Because the universe, your children, your husband, the dog, your car, your body, your in-laws will all see this as a challenge. A dare. They will conspire to ef you up even more. And you will be on your period when it all goes down.

We are going to get older, and so are the kids. Pretty soon, they will be preteens and then teens and then people who think they're adults. When that happens we are going to need more laughs. We are going to hold each other tight and our wineglasses tighter. And, we suspect, we'll have to keep lowering our expectations for ourselves and each other. On good days and bad, grab hold of your friends. They are your lifeline and you are theirs.

As we lay in bed, begging our children to let us peel the hardened boogers off their face, knowing that we smell like aged cheddar, we also know it's all a wonderful gift. We laugh, we cry, we shake our heads, we use sailor words—all before 8:00 a.m. We know these magical monsters will make us remember their tiny chins, the smell of their heads, and the sound of their laughs in the next life.

Challenge accepted.

Godspeed, moms.

ACKNOWLEDGMENTS

Neither one of us has ever run a marathon, but we've seen them on TV and we have been there to support our friends who have run. You know how there are people standing on the side with paper cups of water or energy gel (gross) so the runners can get a little refresher to keep them going? That's how it feels when you get the opportunity to write a book and you have a great team of people who support you, guide you, and see you through to the finish line. At every turn, we have had someone holding a metaphorical paper cup of water, or cheering us on, and even giving us that extra push to say, *You can do this!* To all of those folks, we say, *Thank you.*

Hilary Swanson, our fearless editor at HarperCollins, and the entire HarperOne team, especially Sydney Rogers, we are so incredibly grateful that you had the confidence in us to write this book. So many people underestimate or overlook moms, but Hilary, you saw us and you let us BE us. Thank you for your passion, your guidance, and most of all, your kindness. You are a real champion for women.

ACKNOWLEDGMENTS

We would like to thank Becky Cole, who was absolutely our coach during this writing process. You are a gift. You kept us in line, on schedule, and on track and pushed us to explore things that were scary and emotional, and we are so glad we did. Working with you made us better writers, and we are incredibly grateful for your patience and editorial wizardry.

We would also like to express our gratitude to all our agents at UTA in Los Angeles and in New York. We know there is a monumental amount of work behind the scenes and we want to say thank you to all of the agents, assistants, and even the nice valet guys who make it possible for us to live out our dreams. Thank you for being patient with us and for the occasional kick in the seat. We know you are rooting for us. We feel like you are family (and we mean that in a good way).

A special thank-you to our Hannah. You are welcome for your awesome job. Hannah Myers, we know you get stuck with the un-fun stuff like organizing our schedules, ordering lunches, planning travel, and on occasion, setting out our Spanx and then digging sweaty microphones out of them after a show. You do it with grace. Without you, we would be lost. (Like, we literally wouldn't know what city we are in, or how to get to where we need to be.) We love you, Hannie!

Matt Feil, our trusted attorney and dear friend, we know how lucky we are to have you! We love you for the bulldog that you are and the teddy bear we know you to be. You are the first person who believed in us, and these Nebraska girls will always remember that. Thank you to you and your lovely wife (Karen) who shares you with us—and especially for bringing over the yummiest homemade hooch ever for Christmas.

Kristin here: To my husband, Colin Sweeney, thank you for letting me talk openly about all things marriage. I'm really glad we got hitched. You have given me all the best parts of my life. To my kids, Finn and Eleanor, thank you for giving me endless material to draw from, but mostly thank you for being two happy little creatures who are a blast to be around. I love you more than my new rug, and you know how much I love that rug. I'd like to give a shout-out to some special lady friends: Laura Davis, Alli Bell, Lynn Haughton, and Danelle Weeder, and a special cheers to my friend Brandy Schott (I really wish you were here and I miss you every day). I would like to thank my siblings, Matthew and Megan. Megan, you always answer when I call, and that's often. And to my parents—my papa, Dewey, your voice calms me and makes me feel brave, and Mom, you are the first blonde I've ever loved. Thank you both for having an incredible sense of humor and teaching me that life is way more fun when you are playful.

Jen here: Dash and Delilah, you are everything. You are boogie-nosed answered prayers and the most joy I've ever known. Nothing else matters. To Jeff, Barb, and Jerry, there has never been a day that I haven't loved you, even when I'm a real pain. Thank you. Mimi and Pappy, keep sending me butterflies. Mandy, Jenny, Missy, and Angie, thanks for teaching me what friendship is. Bobbye Lou, you made a good one. Well done. Brit, thank you for wanting me to have this and believing I could. That's you, in a nutshell. X

There are so many ladies, like a crazy number of ladies, we should thank! God bless you for keeping us sane, honest, grounded, and inspired. Danielle, Diane, Michelle, Lexi, Renée,

ACKNOWLEDGMENTS

Bridget, Dana, Wendy, Erin, Susan, Mia, Nickole, Amanda, Joanna, Monique, Eleanor, Lauren, and Anna. Lady-boss supreme: Sarah Jarrell. And there are some guys, too. Do you know Brit and Colin, our husbands, help make these videos and live shows happen? (They also made our babies happen.) There are a few more dudes that have given us loads of love and support: Ruben, Daniel, Addison, Brent, Michael, Jerad, and all the Westside Comedy guys who lent us their stage. Thank you.

On behalf of both of us, we would like to thank THE MOMS. We read the comments, we read your messages, we feel your love. We have been lucky to meet some of you face-to-face, and you never cease to amaze us. We met a mom who told us at a show that she had not been out with friends in four years and she made it out to see us. *Us!* There was a group of moms who decided to tailgate in Santa Rosa who had chilled white wine and a frittata on the menu, because moms do it best. We have met some of you who were really sick and you showed up anyway. And we are humbled when we think of people like our friend Lauren, who lost her little girl, Hazel, to pediatric cancer. She gets up every day, puts one foot in front of the other, and moves forward even when it feels impossible. You inspire us.

Our whole community of moms inspires us because when we posted a swimsuits video that everybody in their cousin watched, there were almost zero negative or harsh comments about us or the other pictures moms bravely posted. You have proven to us that we, as women, as mothers, as a community, are supportive, thoughtful, hilarious, and a whole lot of fun. Thank you for leading with love. Thank you for reaching out to the military mom who is new to town and very alone, thank you for supporting the mom who is struggling with postpartum with your open and raw experiences with postpartum, and thank you for posting ridiculous pictures your kids drew that are supposed to be rockets and cupcakes but look like wieners and boobs. You inspire us to continue to create and talk openly about the subjects that seem scary and isolating, and YOU push us, to keep going, to keep pushing, to take those extra steps. And sure enough, when we come around the bend we know you are waiting with a large cup of . . . wine. Because you are a true friend. From the deepest part of our hearts we say thank you for making our journey so beautiful. We love you.

TARGET EXCLUSIVE

I TARGET SO HARD

JEN

Target is the only place I work up a sweat. I hit my target heart rate (*bad-oom-cha*). If I have one hour to spend in Target, I fly through there like it's my own home—if my own home was full of throw pillows that actually matched and had a wine aisle. #goals.

When my son was born, I would go to the Target near us that had a grocery store in it. That way when I said, "I have to go to the grocery store," I wasn't lying. Getting even a few minutes alone is such a rarity when you're a new mom. I would go down every aisle, filling my cart with milk, bread, detergent, dry shampoo, and then decorative items: acrylic serving trays, napkin rings, anything in my size Isaac Mizrahi was selling at 30 percent off, wipes, a box of Franzia, and a STARBUCKS

COFFEE THAT I WOULD GET TO FINISH. Then I would head home to apologize for how long I'd been gone, while styling our dining-room table in my head.

I've never gone into Target and bought exactly what I meant to buy. Do I *need* seasonal dish towels? No. I just need clean dish towels, but somehow, one glimpse of those Danish-inspired towels with a tulip on them and I'm seduced. Why do I need light-up signs that say "Cheers"? I don't know, but I do! Target is like a man in a romance novel who works the family ranch. He catches your eye when you should be buying paper towels. He's steady, has everything you need—and all the temptations you don't. He comes in from the prairie all sweaty and dusty and whispers in your ear, "Did you look at the clearance end cap? There's wrapping paper there with coordinating bows and tags. Party plates. Leftover Easter grass. How about I slip some into your . . . cart?" You didn't mean to do it, but you did it. That ranch hand brings me so much joy and makes me feel filthy. In a good way.

There goes the heart rate again. Oh, Target, I just can't quit you.

KRISTIN

Walking into Target is like walking into your neighbor- hood bar, where everybody knows your name. And they're always glad you came.

If you have to take your kids with you to Target, then you will immediately appreciate the joy of a park-once situation. You only have to get out of the car, unload the kids, get a cart, resolve a fight over where everybody is going to sit in the cart, and push until you sweat right into the eye of that bull's-eye ONE TIME. And then when you are done, you only have to load everybody back in, buckle safety seats, unload fourteen bags while screaming idle threats ONE TIME.

Shopping with kids is unnatural. So when I get to go at it alone, I feel like Mother Nature herself is giving me a high five. It's glorious.

The minute I walk in I head straight for the bathroom because, for some reason, Target relaxes me in a way that a steady drip of prune juice cannot. I go in intending to buy dog food and paper towels, but instead of buying what I need, I end up buying what I want and that feels *way* better.

When I go to Target alone, I float. For that hour, I get to be with the better version of me, the one who doesn't yell or scream or cry when her kids decide to turn the mudroom into an actual mud room. I delight. I saunter. I walk through the cosmetics, the latest trends in women's clothing, I pick up some potting soil, cute planters to match, a jumbo box of tampons, and refresh my collection of Farmhouse Modern anything, and I am HAPPY. I wave to anyone wearing a red polo. They like me at Target, and it feels nice to be appreciated—unlike at home. Nobody in Target knows that thirteen minutes ago I was crying in my car while hoovering an entire box of year-old Milk Duds. To those angels in red, I am just a gal, gaily shopping, effortlessly putting blouses, socks, Avengers underwear, orange juice, fruit snacks, six boxes of wine, head bands, an avocado face mask, a Fitbit, a miniature Christmas tree, a bike, three mascaras, and fixings for a homemade pizza into my cart.

When I finally check out, a friendly face, Angie (we're Facebook friends now), starts adding up the "light shopping" I have accomplished. The gentle sound of the scanner "bleeps" with every purchase. *Bleep! Bleep! Bleep!* I'm high on the sounds, thinking, *I did it again.* I walk out, head held high, shoulders back, as I cross the parking lot like *I got this.*

Crap. I forgot the paper towels and dog food.

Looks like I'll just have to go back.